MW01267992

America
United in Hope and Courage

by the Students of the
Rutherford County School System

Write Together Publishing
Nashville, Tennessee

Copyright © 2001 by
Rutherford County Tennessee School System
2240 Southpark Blvd.
Murfreesboro, TN 37128

All rights reserved.

Published by Write Together Publishing ™ LLC.
www.writetogether.com

ISBN   1-931718-15-6 Paperback

Title: America United in Hope and Courage. Multiple Authors.
Subject: Literary Collections, Poetry.

Project Sponsor:
>   Rutherford County Tennessee Board of Education
>   J. Hulon Watson, Superintendent

Project Coordinators:
>   Laura Harper, Assistant Superintendent of Curriculum & Instruction
>   Elizabeth Church, Language Arts Instructional Specialist

Project Design:
>   Jackie Drake, Administrative Assistant

Editors:
>   Laura Harper, Assistant Superintendent of Curriculum & Instruction
>   Elizabeth Church, Language Arts Instructional Specialist
>   Shelia Bratton, Coordinator of Middle Level Instruction
>   Jackie Drake, Administrative Assistant

Art:
>   Cover: Drew Perry, Oakland High School, Grade 12
>   Inside Title: Mac Bydalek, Oakland High School, Grade 11
>   Back Cover: Erin Muehe, Oakland High School, Grade 12

For Write Together Publishing:

Publisher: Paul Clere
Edit-in-Chief: John D. Bauman
Art Director: Bill Perkins
Publishing Coordinator: Michael Pleasant

To publish a book for your school or non-profit organization that complements your academic goals or values, vision and mission, please contact:

Write Together ™ Publishing
533 Inwood Dr.
Nashville, TN 37211

phone: 615-781-1518
fax:520-223-4850
www.writetogether.com

Table of Contents

Chapter 1: Hope and Courage

Chapter 2: America

Chapter 3: The Stars and Stripes

Chapter 4: Letters

Chapter 5: September 11, 2001

Chapter 6: United

RUTHERFORD COUNTY SCHOOLS

2240 Southpark Boulevard
Murfreesboro, Tennessee 37128
Phone (615) 893-5812 • (615) 898-7940

J. Hulon Watson
Superintendent

Dear Students of Rutherford County:

On September 11, 2001 our world, as we knew it, took on another dimension. Our emotional comfort level came into question, and our feelings of safety and security were diminished to the point that we felt little hope for the future of mankind.

Within the pages of *America United in Hope and Courage*, Rutherford County students relay to the reader their hopes and fears, their love of country and their dreams of the future. They share their desire to reestablish not just what was but to create a nation that rises to a higher level of humanity and tolerence of others. As you open the book, you will immediately be swept away by a maturity of thought and expression beyond what most people expect from their young minds.

Thank you to our young writers and artists for grounding us in what really matters most, a secure feeling that our future is safe and in the hands of gifted thinkers and talented leaders who know what is right and who are willing to take a stand and make a mark for all mankind. We are united in our hope for the future and supported by the courage of all Americans.

Sincerely,

J. Hulon Watson
Superintendent of Schools

Alana Scudder
Oakland High School, Grade 12

Chapter 1
Hope and Courage

America United in Hope and Courage

Suzannah Applis Molloy
Homer Pittard Campus School, Grade 6

The bald eagle soared over the flames and wreckage of what had been, and three big tears rolled down her feathered cheek. They fell, quenching flames that hissed loudly as they were put out. The eagle looked down and saw Liberty stooped over, her dress dirty with ashes, her tear-streaked cheeks glistening in the sunlight. Beside her feet lay the torch, its faintly glowing flame sputtering softly. Liberty picked it up and with her warm breath blew the flame back to life. It slowly but steadily regained its orange-hot strength. As it burned brightly, it dried the tears on Liberty's cheeks. She grasped the torch firmly and strode back to her platform, beacon of the free. The eagle released her fierce, wild cry, "Liberty and freedom still reign!" A little dove heard and cooed, reminding us in its small way that peace would be gained.

★
1

America United in Hope and Courage
Alex Pegram
Oakland High School, Grade 9

As the world watches
America is attacked by indescribable evil
Fear swells in the hearts of millions
Friendships lost
Families destroyed
Lives taken
America persists
America continues
Unified by hope and courage
America stands tall and strong
Liberated and proud
One nation under God

In the Beginning
Benjamin Bearden
David Youree Elementary School, Grade 5

In the beginning we won our freedom from Great Britain. Then came slavery in the South. On that day we began to fight. Now *everyone* has certain rights. I'm glad that we have these rights, such as freedom of speech, and that everyone is treated equally. Sometimes I think of all the people that died for those rights. Now, we stand united in true hope and courage. I believe that we are truly united. Now, we stand united against the terrorists who want to end our freedoms. Now we will see what a great nation we are.

Above and Beyond
James Spires
Oakland High School, Grade 9

Through the pain and strife
High above an eagle flies
Will its path be yours?

★
2

Courage
Ashley Wardlaw
LaVergne High School, Grade 10

America, we stand free.
Proud of our country,
Americans we'll always be.

With hope and courage
We stand by our name.
America our country
Carries all of the fame.

Courage will represent our flag.
Hope will get us through good times and bad.

America United by Hope and Courage
Emily Mitchell
Oakland High School, Grade 9

Like soldiers marching to their destiny,
Numerous firemen ascended the stairs.
We will never forget those who went up
When everyone else was coming down.
Their fate whirled around them,
A cloud of smoke before their eyes,
Scalding, blistering, intense burning.
Around them the consumed remains crashed down.
Like soldiers they died for their country.
They died so that others might live.
They died putting out the fire,
And now the fire burns in our hearts.
It burns with fury, rage, courage
Uncertainty, and hope.
Earth has its ashes and heaven its heart.

★

United in Hope and Courage

Hannah McKinney
Oakland High School, Grade 9

I am from a country in war.
A country under attack
From a country sending men off to war
From a country united in hope and courage

I am from a country in mourning.
In mourning for the death of family and friends
From a country full of lost loved ones
From a country united in hope and courage

I am from a country hit with tragedy.
From burning buildings, crashing planes, to workers jumping in pairs
From a country terrorized by hijackers
From a country united in hope and courage

I am from a country in prayer.
Praying for our military leaders
From a country that prays we are on God's side
From a country united in hope and courage

I am from a strong country.
From a nation no one can tear apart
From a country united in hope and courage
AMERICA

Stars and Stripes Are Forever

Elizabeth Wade
Cedar Grove Elementary, Grade 4

We, the people of the United States,
Know the bitter fruits of hate.
Although our hearts are full of sorrow,
We still believe in a bright tomorrow.
We are united in hope and prayer.
Our courage and dreams we won't forbear.
Our motto is "In God We Trust."
For the land of the free, this is a must.
Stars and Stripes are forever,
And we will stand together.
We Are United
In Hope And Courage.

★

America United In Hope and Courage

Jack Richmond
Oakland High School, Grade 11

"These are the times that try men's souls." The words of Thomas Paine from *The Crisis, No. 1* have found new meaning for Americans in the wake of the September 11 attacks on our country. Today, as in the American Revolution, the United States is once again fighting for freedom. Now, we fight not against oppressive foreign dominion, but to emancipate our country from fear. The pusillanimous acts of September 11 may have destroyed buildings and taken lives, but the American spirit persevered, bolder and stronger. The villains who hijacked our planes hoped to topple American will and change our way of life, while in fact they have done the opposite.

Like never before, Americans stand united as one, a paragon of nationalism and pride. Patriotism is rampant throughout the country; flags are displayed ubiquitously, from flagpoles to baseball caps, from cars to clothing. Generosity is prevalent in society, as evidenced by the munificent gifts made to the Red Cross, United Way, and other worthy causes. Policemen and firemen are hailed as national heroes, and the nation has come together behind our president and armed forces as they try to bring the heartless perpetrators of the attacks to justice.

A Japanese admiral said after the bombing of Pearl Harbor, "I fear that we have only served to awaken a sleeping giant." The same is true now. Not only was the "giant" of American military power awakened, but also the indomitable American spirit, which no amount of strife can extinguish. "The harder the conflict, the more glorious the victory." Paine's words again ring true. Although the battle may be long, terrorism will not stand. The struggles and losses of the present will always be remembered, but they will pave the way for an assured, glorious future for the people of this great land.

A Ray of Hope

Daniel Mosse'
Blackman High School, Grade 9

An ancient proverb has come to say,
"A misty morning does not signify a cloudy day."
Through the darkness a light has shone
On the victims of violence I cannot condone.

★

5

Americans

Katie Gray
Cedar Grove Elementary School, Grade 7

It was in the sorrow
We saw a little light.
And it was in the sadness
We knew it would be all right.

It was in the tragedy,
But we saw it all,
And anyone could help,
No matter how big or how small.

It was in the anger
We knew to forgive each other.
We all came together like lifelong
Sisters and brothers.

We are Americans,
We'll stand firm to the end.
And to all the lost souls
Our blessing we send.

Americans from all over,
We unite.
And through it all,
We will win the fight.

America United in Hope and Courage

Mary Allen
Oakland High School, Grade 9

No one expected it.
It happened in an instant.
After it, everything changed.
Now, no one is the same.
Everyone has been affected in some way.

It is not…the threats, attacks, or death that has damaged our country.
It is…the empowerment of pride and faith our country is showing.
It is not…the American flags on every car and every yard.
It is…the way we act toward each other with kindness and gratitude.

★

6

Americans once again live each day with the hope and courage
That our nation will overcome this horrible tragedy.

United in Hope and Courage
Margaret Parham
Cedar Grove Elementary School, Grade 5

I have hopes
Hopes in people finding others
Hopes in policemen, firemen, and rescue squad members
Hopes that they will remain faithful.

I have hopes
Hopes for people who lost a loved one
A brother, sister, mom, dad, or friend
I have hopes that they will stay strong.

I have courage
Courage in soldiers who will fight
They will fight to win in war
They will fight for our country.

I have courage
Courage to ride in planes
Planes that won't crash
They won't crash into buildings
Buildings like the Twin Towers and the Pentagon.

I give thanks
Thanks for the people who will risk their lives for others
Special people
People like you and me.

God Bless Us All

Heart of an Army

Kyle Cantrell
Blackman High School, Grade 9

With the wind in his hair
And hope in his heart
He goes into the field of battle
Fighting to keep our freedom
This isn't just the story of one
But the story of many
Who are in the army of one
And in that army there are many hearts of hope
And many hearts of courage
When the army is in battle
All those hearts become one
And go out to fight for freedom
All the enemy can hear is the beating of that heart
The beating will never go away
Because hope and courage will never die.

Hope and Courage

Zach Norton
Smyrna Elementary School, Grade 4

People who believe in things have hopes and dreams. These hopes are real.
People who make things right when they are wrong have courage to do what has to
be done and hope that it will work out. That's what makes this country very great —
hope and courage.

America United in Hope and Courage

Ashley Caldwell
Smyrna Middle School, Grade 7

In order to survive and stand together, we need to continue to have hope, courage, and strength. Having hope will help us make it through difficult times. To live in a country that has so much courage makes me proud. Within this strong country, we will stay united. Eventually these three things will make us a better country.

As we keep our hope in this present situation, we will show how we can win this war to stop terrorism. I believe we should go on with our daily lives and hope that this is only a temporary situation. I think hope is contagious. If one person has hope, then they can pass it on to another. All we need to do to retain our hope is to keep passing it from person to person.

We also need courage. Whenever someone says courage, I think of the lion in *The Wizard of Oz*. He thought he didn't have courage, but hoped that the wizard would give it to him. He found that he already had courage, but just didn't show it because he was too worried about being scared. The United States military men have no choice; they must use courage to survive. Often there is no time to be scared or worried. They just have to be ready.

Strength is also needed at this time. Thinking of strength makes me remember how it looked to watch the tapes of the terrorists striking the Trade Towers. I also think of strength when the news programs run films showing the people of Afghanistan, especially the children, leaving their homes. Strength is very important to have and is not always about power; sometimes it is about just doing what must be done. If our country did not have strength, we could not survive.

In conclusion, we need to combine hope, courage and strength. When you think of it, you must have hope to have courage. You must have courage to have strength. This will help us stand together and stay united. If we stay united, we will win this war and stop terrorism.

The Stranger's Hand

Katie Logan
Riverdale High School, Grade 10

The early morning sun danced across the ground as I inched my car a bit closer to the bumper of the jeep in front of me. I glanced over at my mother as she studied her time sheets for work. She hardly noticed the radio buzzing through the car. And it was not the usual morning talk show banter I had grown accustomed to hearing while sitting in traffic on my way to school. No, the talk on that particular day, September 14, 2001, was centered on the tragic events that had taken place several days before. The terrorist attacks on the United States were the hot topic of every radio and television show.

I chewed my lip and tried to concentrate on driving. The radio continued to drone in my ears. "Patriotism," the host offered for discussion. "What does it really mean to be patriotic?"

My ears perked up, and I swallowed hard. I wondered, too. The first thing that came to mind was the national anthem, and second, the flag. So, I could sing the national anthem whenever I had the chance, and place American flags on all my belongings, and…

My thoughts trailed off. Somehow, it wasn't enough. As I steered my car towards the front of the school, I delved deep into the recesses of my mind and questioned my own thoughts. What does it mean to be patriotic? What does it mean to be united? What does it mean to have hope?

If someone had walked up to me during school and asked me any one of these three questions, I would have been stumped; and being a teenager, I would have simply shrugged and laughed it off. I wouldn't know what to think of such a question.

I stopped by the entrance to my high school and put the car in park. My mother climbed out of her seat in pursuit of mine. I smiled at her as I walked around the green automobile. "Bye," I said gently, as always.

"Have a great day, Katie." She replied cheerfully.

"I'll try," I sighed dramatically as I spoke, and her smile broadened.

I turned and walked the few feet to the doors, running a hand through my hair. I found my fingers tangled within the curls and had to twist them out carefully. It was difficult, but I eventually pulled free and groaned at my ignorance. Not only was I annoyed by my hair, but also by the question I could not answer.

What is patriotism?

My feet clicked on the hard floor of the school. I found it strange that I could hear my steps and noticed the peculiar absence of the usual roar of cheerful students. I walked more slowly, almost alarmed to find no one lining the hallway on the way to the cafeteria. All students were supposed to stay in the cafeteria before the bell rang in the mornings, but usually a number waited in the hallway to avoid the big, open space.

I swallowed and stepped into the cafeteria…

…and stumbled upon the location of the missing students.

★

They stood in an oddly shaped circle, several rows thick. I was shocked to hear very little noise even here, with an inestimable number of students gathered in close quarters. There were no teachers, no coaches, no adults for that matter, just teenagers with their heads bowed and their eyes lowered. I remained frozen, unsure of how to react.

"Katie! Over here!"

I found the source of the voice and smiled. My friend waved for me to join her, so I put my things on the table and interrupted the circle. I automatically took the familiar girl's hand.

Turning to the person on the other side of me, I found that his hand was already open and waiting for mine. I stared at his open palm for a moment. He was a complete stranger; however, he was still eager to invite me in.

In that moment I found the answer to my question. It was like trying to untangle my fingers from my hair. The solution was simple, but I had to struggle to find it.

Patriotism isn't just carrying an American flag or wearing red, white, and blue. It is the willingness to accept a stranger and the freedom to do so. Patriotism means to stand united not only with friends and family, but also with strangers.

As I stood there, the stranger's hand suddenly meant so much more to me. I smiled as I bowed my head and placed my hand in his.

United we stood in support of our crippled country.

And united we prayed for the hope we needed to carry on.

Untitled

Nate Shoptaw
LaVergne High School, Grade 12

The bald eagle flies high.
He flies high in the blue sky.
He flies over the grass so green.
Everything so beautiful he has seen,
The mountain, rock, and deep blue seas,
The flowing river and tall, green trees,
The smooth beaches and grassy plains,
The gentle hills and cool rains.
A shot rings out through the air,
The eagle's wing has a tear.
He falters in his strong flight,
He begins to fall from that great height.
But strength is with him as he stops his fall.
He begins to rise without stall.
He signifies with a great cry,
"I will not fall and I will not die!"

★

America United in Hope and Courage

Victoria Britton
Blackman High School, Grade 12

I was born into a life of freedom. I have never had to worry that men with guns would come into my home at night and execute me for being female. I have never been forced to hide my face and silence my every thought and feeling out of fear for my existence. There was a time when such a place, where people were executed without cause or reason, seemed very far away. Now, that place feels entirely too close to home.

Until two months ago, I looked at saying the Pledge of Allegiance in school as a nuisance and a hassle. I could not understand why it was deemed necessary that every day we should stand up and mumble aloud a mass of words that lost their meaning a long time ago. I took for granted the freedom that I had even to recite the pledge. I had not considered the fact that if someone was hungry, there was food to be had. I took for granted the fact that I had never had to pass a soldier with a machine gun in the street, nor felt my breath catch in my throat as I wondered if perhaps today he would decide to kill me next.

On September 11, 2001 I sat in my economics class and took not only the freedom that my country has given me for granted, but also life itself. It wasn't until I sat there, stunned beyond belief, that I suddenly realized terrorism and fear were in my country, in my home. It was not until that moment that I was able to appreciate the pain and the absolute horror that so many people all over the world have felt their entire lives. It did not occur to me to give thanks for the freedoms that I have until I realized that my nation is not invincible, and that however horrifying the idea might be, it is not completely out of the realm of possibility to imagine that our nation could be demolished.

All over the United States there has been a powerful surge of patriotism that has charged men, women, and children alike to stand together as a nation and refuse to surrender everything that our ancestors spent their lives trying to accomplish. The road to freedom and justice in America has been a long one, and it's not yet complete. But now that we have known tragedy, we are united on that path, and we refuse to quit that path.

Those who once verbally abused the President now mumble words of encouragement as our President stands leading us into a battle where the signs of victory are often blurry, while the signs of defeat are painfully clear. A pessimistic attitude towards both our country and our leaders is no longer prevalent among Americans. We have instead adopted a much more admirable attitude of hope. We truly believe that we can defeat the seemingly invincible, and right the wrongs that have affected so many. Perhaps it is our unfaltering faith and courage that will be the key weapons in preserving everything that we have worked to attain.

One cannot help but believe that in the end, our hope and our courage as a nation will guide us through all of the conflicts that are still foremost in our minds. I have never been more moved than when I realized how many people risked their lives to save others as the World Trade Center towers fell around them. Upon realizing that it was intended by terrorists that thousands of innocent people be killed senselessly, I found myself ashamed to be a member of the human race. It is incomprehensible to me that one might choose to inflict that kind of pain on so many people. And for what purpose? I sat and I watched as everything that I had known my entire life was changing. As I sat, consumed by feelings of despair and confusion, I began to listen. Over the next few days, I heard story after story about the lengths that the people in the Trade Center went to in order to try to save each other. As I listened to those people's stories, my faith in humanity was restored. So many gave their lives so that others could live. Running into a crumbling, demolished building, knowing you probably won't come back out yet risking it all in the hopes of saving someone is the very definition of courage. Standing up when we could sit back in horror and allow our country to be desecrated by terrorists requires courage. Believing that we can win this battle, regardless of what may happen, is hope. In a matter of hours, I saw more patriotism emerge than I had seen in the entirety of my seventeen years. We are America. We will not be defeated. We are united…in hope, and in courage…and we will endure.

America United in Hope and Courage

Kelly Colvert
Oakland High School, Grade 11

United we stand,
United we speak,
But really and truly,
United are we?

We do stand strong,
Stand even the weak,
And really and truly,
United are we.

We stand not alone,
We stand without fear,
We have stood,
We will stand from year to year.

America the beautiful,
America the great,
The land of the free,
Every last state.

Tragedy comes,
Tragedy goes,
United we stand,
Sun high and sun low.

United we stand,
United we speak,
But really and truly,
United are we?

We do stand strong,
Stand even the weak,
And really and truly,
United are we.

We
Stand
united
together

Brittany Butler
Central Middle School, Grade 8

Chapter 2
America

America United in Hope and Courage

Courtney Davis
Smyrna Primary School, Grade 4

Answering through hope and courage.
Mending a melting pot into one nation.
Emerging strong and encouraging each other.
Remembering and hoping together.
Instilling hope through helping hands.
Coming to aid all mankind.
America!

America

Donna Shoults
Oakland High School, Grade 9

America
filled   *with*
hopes   *and*
dreams.   *Loving*
and   *caring*
families   *who*
have lost many loved ones
throughout   *the*
years.   *America*
with   *its hopes*
and   *courage*
has   *finally*
come   *together*
as   *one.*

America the Free

Matt Houglum
Christiana Elementary School, Grade 6

America the magnificent,
Where there's new hope every day.
America the magnificent,
Where they can't take freedom away.
America the marvelous,
Whose patriotism you can see.
America the marvelous,
That's where I'm proud to be.
America the wonderful,
Where many men have died,
But only to defend
Our wonderful nation's pride.
America the beautiful,
God shed his grace on thee.
America the beautiful,
America the free.

America United in Hope and Courage

Braden Hunsicker
Cedar Grove Elementary School, Grade 3

America united in hope and courage equals bravery, taking care of each other, working as teammates, being friends, loving, being free, being your best, honesty, fairness, helpfulness, kindness, and having a pure heart.

America's Poem

Savannah Gentry
Smyrna West Kindergarten

I hope we have a good day today.
I hope we have a good day tomorrow.
America is strong.
People are nice.
Some days were sad.
Tomorrow will be great!
We hope nothing else bad happens to our country.
America is great and we will be brave.
We hope it is a good day in America tomorrow!

★

The Great Place

Kelsey Delemar
Smyrna Primary School, Grade 2

America, America, it's the place you want to see.
America, America, it's the place you want to be.
It makes you smile, it makes you laugh.
You can do what you want, just ask.
America, America, it's so beautiful.
Can't you see?
It's the place that everyone wants to be.
And I will never, oh, never leave.
This very good place.
This place is great for me!

My Country

Collin Smith
McFadden School of Excellence, Grade 3

America, America
How nice you are
From north to south
And east to west.
America has many different people
From countries around the world.
Whatever happens, still we are strong.
From every state to every town,
We still move on.

America United in Hope and Courage

Zac Cox
Thurman Francis School, Grade 4

America is united.
My country is free.
Everyone is welcome.
Reliable as we are, you can trust us.
In America, you will be happy.
Come, come.
America is united.

★

America United in Hope and Courage

Andrew Mitchell
Wilson Elementary School, Grade 5

While other countries stand, whither, and fall, we glance to see America standing tall. While others fall to their knees and cry, America comes to lift them high. When light no longer shines, America comes in time and drives the evil away. Our flag is waving gallantly on to this day. We are "the land of the free and the home of the brave."

America Is

Bethany Watson
Cedar Grove Elementary School, Grade 7

America is home of the red, white, and blue.
America is home of the free.
When in America, all is true.
America is where I want to be.

America is one body, heart, and soul
With many different faces.
All the individuals are part of a whole
Living in many different places.

America Is Free

Katie Ezell
David Youree Elementary School, Grade 1

The United States is our home. We should protect and take care of it. It is God's creation and we should respect it. We should help and respect each other. I hope that everybody has enough courage to turn their backs on evil and keep America *free!*

★

America Stands Tall!

Grace Dodson
Lascassas Elementary School, Grade 3

Buildings may fall,
But American stands tall.

Our flag still waves
Over this great land
As we work and play
Hand in hand!

Brave men and women
And children too
Stand for freedom,
For me and you!

We wave our flags
Together as one
As we work, play,
And as we have fun!

Buildings may fall,
But America stands tall!

America

James Hill
Lascassas Elementary School, Grade 4

America
free, beautiful
loving, uniting, helping
flag, freedom, President, man
thinking, planning, caring
brave, courageous
George Bush

★

America Will Still Stand Tall

Casey Edwards
Siegel Middle School, Grade 6

The flag of red, white, and blue
Stands very high and very true

Our freedom may never be taken
Though buildings were rattled and shaken

Though bricks and concrete fall
The Statue of Liberty stands tall

Our country sits on eagle wings
Through our troubles freedom rings

America is strong
Through things that are very wrong

In America justice is done
We will fight till peace is won

America

Morgan Pennington
Lascassas Elementary School, Grade 4

America
hopeful, nice
loving, caring, hoping
George Bush, Uncle Sam, towers, people
helping, crashing, saving
big, busy
New York

Freedom

Jacob Cannady
Wilson Elementary School, Grade 3

We live in a place where the sun shines
In a place where we can fly our flags
Where we can say we are Americans
Where we can be proud of who we are

We are free.

United States

Ryan Smoot
Siegel Middle School, Grade 6

United States
Beautiful, awesome
Helping, caring, cheering
The   home   for   many
Enlightening, winning, loving
Free, peaceful
America

America Stands United

Jordan Davis
Barfield Elementary School, Grade 4

Living in America and being an American citizen are very important to me because we have the freedom to do many things.

I am free to watch a football game without the government's consent, and I have the right to get an education. I feel safe in America because I depend on heroes such as firemen and policemen to protect me.

America stands for courage and love and stands united. This is why I am proud to be an American.

★

American Cinquain
Wilmesha Cowan
John Colemon Elementary School, Grade 4

New York
Sad, lonely
Falling, crying, digging
Scared, frightened
Brave

American Cinquain
Nick Dwyer
John Colemon Elementary School, Grade 4

Heroes
Scared, hurt
Finding, helping, saving
Crying, hurt
Police

America
Matthew Reed
Lascassas Elementary School, Grade 4

America
peaceful, colorful
helping, giving, caring
President, flag, Bible, faith
fighting, praying, uniting
brave, courageous
People

★
23

America United in Hope and Courage
Peetie Webster
Siegel Middle School, Grade 6

America, where freedom rings
And people sing of unity and love
With hope for the future and blue skies above...
Where courage is found every day to face the evil and terrorism others display
America will stand united, hopeful, and courageous
In God we pray.

Freedom
Jewel Mariah Bess
Blackman High School, Grade 10

Warm and shining bright
Freedom in the horizon
Can you feel the warmth?

America
Christina Wells
Lascassas Elementary School, Grade 4

America
peaceful, beautiful
loving, helping, singing
flag, freedom, helmet, uniform
saving, fighting, helping
strong, brave
Soldiers

America United in Hope and Courage
Heather Hill
Buchanan Elementary School, Grade 8

America is a place where people can be free.
Immigrants can come here and they don't need a key.
★ America always stands tall and strong

Even when other countries do us wrong.
Even at times of war and hate
Old Glory still stands tall and straight.
In times of great tragedy and terrible fear,
Americans join hands and volunteer.
America's hope and courage will always stand true
Because it is woven into our flag with red, white, and blue.

America United in Hope and Courage
Jacob Gibbs
Cedar Grove School, Grade 8

When you think of America, what do you picture in your mind? My mind portrays a land of the free and home of the brave. But America did not become free by sitting around and being lazy. Thanks to bold citizens willing to fight for their country and their desire for a better world, America has become the greatest nation worldwide.

Throughout history, Americans have proven to the world that they have the qualities that it takes to be a strong nation. Since the Revolutionary War, American men, women, and children have united together in a common cause to rise above all other nations.

Further on in America's history, during the Vietnam War, Americans proved that they are willing to aid other countries in achieving a common goal—peace. This isn't the only country that we have helped. We have also aided Israel, Korea, Bosnia, and Iraq. If it takes courage to fight for your country, then it takes even more to help others when they need it. This demands trust that our higher ranked officials will make the right decisions.

Today we are struggling to keep our dream of peace and freedom alive and to maintain our valor. Since the recent terrorist attacks, America is struggling to keep her confidence alive. Because of loyal and heroic firefighters, many of those once missing under the Twin Towers are now alive. On the battlefields of Afghanistan, fearless troops fight to keep freedom's fire alight. America is coming together, yet again, as a united nation.

We have conquered before, are fighting now, and will forever triumph over evil as long as the American people have hope. In the darkest of situations, hope provides light and a way out. As long as the American nation has confidence in itself, brave souls will emerge with new strengths, conquering evil. United we are strong.

★

America United in Hope and Courage

Jeri Lynn Cokeroft
Cedar Grove Elementary School, Grade 6

Each and every day, our school recites a creed,
And when I think about it, I picture those in need.

Inside I want to help them as much as I possibly can.
To reach, touch, and care for them, to lend a helping hand.

Clothing, food, and shelter are some things that we can give,
But love, peace, and caring, too, are what they need to live.

America was founded on these things, we understand,
Faith in God, pride in country, and a love for fellow man.

So place the needs of others far above those of your own.
The flag of freedom will remain as the greatest ever flown.

America Stands for Freedom

Stephen Barrett
Eagleville School, Grade 6

America offers hope to people to live free and not be judged by the way they look or their religion. When America is threatened, we join together and defend the freedom we have. We show the world that we are united and have the courage to stand up for what we believe. America is the best country in the world, and we should be thankful to live here.

God Bless America

Katy Patterson
Lascassas Elementary School, Grade 6

God bless America,
The mighty U.S.A.
God bless America,
Where we have the right to pray.
God bless America,
Land of the free.
God blessed America,
Just for you and me.

★

America

Taylor Watson
McFadden School of Excellence, Grade 5

Always willing to help those in need
Multiple opportunities
Everyone counts
Ready to defend freedom
I can be anything I want
Caring for everyone
America is a beautiful country and I would not want to live anywhere else.

America

Brittany Edwards
Wilson Elementary School, Grade 4

Families
Strong, determined,
Loving, trusting, waiting
We will stand united,
Empowered.

America Is My Home

Brittany Drumpus
Thurman Francis School, Grade 5

America is my home, not any other.
It is the place I want to be.
It is the place where we are free.
If we stand united and have courage,
We will always be that way.
And everyone is different,
Some people are white, black, or brown.
But, there is one way we are the same—
We all live in America!

America

Alexanna Murphy
McFadden School of Excellence, Grade 5

America
Protected, secure
Learning, working, living
Peace, justice, war, injustice
Crashing, fleeing, dying
Vulnerable, angry
America

Faith

Latelia Wade
LaVergne High School, Grade 10

As I look around at everything
I used to know and used to feel,
I take a deep breath and wish things that
Happened hadn't, that they were not real.

I dare not turn on the television for comfort.
It does not ease the pain.
It only magnifies my sorrow and turns
A sunny day into rain.

So here I sit engulfed with hidden hate
Unable to seize the day,
Trying to keep positive thoughts in my life
Keeping an open mind so that they may.

Yet I'm still unable to surmount this disastrous situation.
I pray that it is not a prelude of what is to come.
I, heartbroken, not understanding how
Someone else's soul can become so numb.

I offer my hand to my united country.
I keep faith during these times that try men's souls,
Understanding just why my ancestors were willing
To sacrifice their honor, lives, silver, and gold.

Proud to live in America,
Happy that it is the land of the free.
Shouting GOD BLESS AMERICA,
The land of life, love, and liberty.

America the Brave
Marilyn Jackson
McFadden School of Excellence, Grade 1

America, America,
Together we are not scared.
We help each other when we are hurt.
America, America,
We stand!

America United
Sterling Scruggs
Wilson Elementary School, Grade 4

We are united and strong.
We will stand as we go on!

We are prepared and we have hope.
We have courage to win the war!

Deep down in my heart I love America so much!
I will never forget September 11!

America—united, strong, and hopeful!

America United in Hope and Courage
Jennifer Jones
Stewartsboro Elementary School, Grade 4

America is united in hope and courage. Who knows what will happen in the weeks, months, and years to come? Will our country be able to survive the horror, terror and fear of war? Who would have ever thought that September 11, 2001 would turn out to be a day of terror?

In a single day millions of people who were filled with love and happiness in an instant were turned to terror. I can't imagine the horror and fear the people must have felt as the planes they were on crashed into America's famous landmarks. Although the attacks took place on the World Trade Center, on the Pentagon, and in a Pennsylvania field, the attacks affected every U.S. citizen.

As the flames burned for days, the world seemed to come closer together. As Americans face the coming days, we must help one another during this crisis. People in every country knew that the world would never be the same. This is one of the few days in life that will actually affect everything as we know it. By coming together, Americans can and will grow and become stronger than ever.

★
29

America coniuncta in spe et virtute
Brittany and Natalie Martin
Oakland High School, Grade 10

Verba manent – inustra in mentem meam
Similis soli qui coloribus caelum maculat
Nuntius salutis evanescentis nostrae
Tandem populus e somnio lento exitat
Distracti scissique a terrae motu
Convenimus reponentes partes
Solum firmi sine odio reparare possunt
Piget recordari sed omnes illa die
In America unus facti sunt
Stellae lucidius lucedere videntur

America United in Hope and Courage

Brittany and Natalie Martin
Oakland High School, Grade 10

The words remain – branded into my mind
Like the sun stains the sky with its colors
The news of our disappearing security
Finally people awake from their apathetic dreams
Torn and ripped apart by this earthquake
We come together placing the pieces back
Only the strong can rebuild without hate
To remember is painful but on that day everyone in America became one
The stars seem to shine brighter

(English translation of Latin poem on preceding page)

America United in Hope and Courage
Sean Torres
Smyrna Primary School, Grade 4

America, America from your rolling hills
To your oceans blue
That are so beautiful and true
From New York to California your strength is mighty true
Your children will stand beside you fighting off the wolves
Your strength will come from their courage
Our hope will never fade for it is strong too
How beautiful our flag and how strong we are too.

America United in Hope and Courage
Katie Nutt
Rockvale Elementary School, Grade 8

With reds and whites, and stars and stripes,
Through which our freedom rings,
Inside the strong, eternal song,
That every color brings.

Within the gentle waves of blue,
The ever-glowing stars,
There stands a lasting promise,
A right that's only ours.

When they tried to tear away
The freedom in our heart,
We wouldn't let them crush the clay
Or tear us all apart.

We've risen even higher
Even though we fell,
So now we work together.
Our strength, we cannot tell.

They can never leave our grasp,
Trapped within their hate.
And since they caused such spiteful pain,
They'll suffer a worse fate.

★

America, the Home of the Brave

Lauren Allison Rigsby
Rockvale Elementary School, Grade 6

Though America is a fairly young country, compared to some others, we have established a great nation. America is open and welcoming to those who seek freedom and liberty. The ruthless attack on September 11, 2001 was meant to weaken us, but instead we are strengthened in heart, mind, and soul. We are unified even greater than ever before, but with grief and anger. It is important that we are united in hope, courage, and brotherhood.

It is important that we have hope. Hope is a trait that helps us manage tough times. If our country had no hope, where would we be today? If we hope and believe that our country will defeat terrorism and other evils, we will conquer them. We should set an example of how to overcome terrorism, and maybe other countries will follow our lead.

If we have courage, America will stand strong. Even if fear is brought to our country, we will resist it. There are a lot of courageous people in America that help keep our country together. They sometimes risk their lives. Those people love America a lot, and we should too.

America is joined together in brotherhood. Though we quarrel sometimes, the people of America are still brought together in friendship. We work together to make our country stronger. In unity we can accomplish great things.

It is important that we are united in hope, courage, and brotherhood. America is very tough, and we will make it through lots of hard times. That is why America is my favorite country, my home.

What America Is to Me

Kaitlyn White
Kittrell Elementary School, Grade 3

A is for anybody who can be what they want.
M is for miracle, because that's what America is to me.
E is for everything we share.
R is for righteousness, because that's part of what makes our nation.
I is for I love this country and I hope you do too.
C is for courage, because that's what binds us together.
A is for awesome, because that's what our country is.

America United in Hope and Courage

Dylan LeDoux
Siegel Middle School, Grade 7

Life is precious.
It cannot be wasted.
It cannot be fixed.
It cannot be pasted.

People risked their lives.
It took my breath away.
But America stands tall,
And we will never fall.

It's now time
To stand up and say
Our flag stands for freedom,
And they can't take that away.

America stands tall.
And no one can bring us down.
In the end, we stand tall and proud.
Hope and courage all around.

God bless all Americans!

We Americans

Nikki Douglas
LaVergne High School, Grade 9

In history books, we've read of war.
Now it's here at our front door.

They say to live our lives the same,
But we really can't; we saw those planes!

We know that people are living with fear,
But some things have been made quite clear.

We Americans, we stand tall.
Because of this, we will not fall.

Our American flag – red, white, and blue –
Stands for me and you, and unity too.

In history books they will soon read,
Of faith in God and liberty.
And all Americans are still free.

The Results of Tragedy

Aimee Young
LaVergne High School, Grade 9

Dreams were shattered one by one,
As devastated people saw the damage done.
Their hearts were broken by the sorrowful sight
Of American soldiers marching into the night.
Prayers of the citizens were lifted high,
After seeing fellow Americans grieve and cry.
Still they remain hopeful, united they'll stand,
To lend their neighbors a helping hand.
Though some display evil and keep doing wrong,
Americans take pride, and for their country, sing a song.
Those who do evil will hear and be troubled,
Love will overcome them and any good inside their hearts will be doubled.
America's courage will inspire others to be courageous too,
And have faith that America *will* make it through.

Lady Liberty

Lesley Williams
Lascassas Elementary School, Grade 4

Lady Liberty
tall, pretty
standing, holding, hoping
statue, woman, stars, stripes
waving, whistling, flying
beautiful, colorful
Flag

★
35

America
Morgan Faulkner
Siegel Middle School, Grade 6

America
Strong, loving
Faith we have
People believe in us
We have hope in America
The flag stands high
Freedom we have
Courageous, brave
Beautiful

America United in Hope and Courage
Daniel Sears
Cedar Grove Elementary School, Grade 3

I think being united in hope and courage means helping others. It means being persistent. It means being brave. It means being the best you can be. It means respecting others and not discouraging them. It means being a good friend. It means being loving. It means trying not to be scared. God bless America.

My Country
Jacquelyn Gondolfi
Cedar Grove Elementary School, Grade 6

America, my country,
I salute thee.
A country of pride
And of liberty.

My heart goes out
To those we have lost.
I am dedicated to you
No matter the cost.

Together we must form a band.
Precious America, united we stand.

★

America America

Megan McDonald
Central Middle School, Grade 7

America is held together in hope, courage, and love.
Of all the other countries we stand above.
We're all different, you from me,
And maybe one day they will see
No money, no goods, no anthrax scare
Can tear us apart, but they don't care.
They try to break our hope,
So maybe we won't be able to cope
With all the stuff they try to do
To my family, my friends, to me, and to you.
Some people say they don't know what to do,
But someday I know that we will pull through
Because we are America held together in hope, courage, and love.

Ashley Brown
Central Middle School, Grade 8

Chapter 3
The Stars and Stripes

The American Flag

Ashley Elliott
Cedar Grove Elementary School, Grade 7

When I look at the flag flying softly in the wind,
I feel that our country's unity has come from within.

When I look at the colors red, white, and blue,
I feel that our freedom has become anew.

When I look at the flag, I pause to reflect,
Oh, how I feel like my country and I connect.

I remember all the people whose lives were lost,
Now I realize how much my freedom really cost.

I want to show my gratitude to those whose lives were taken away.
I will remember that is why I have my freedom to this day.

Our Hope in the Flag
Danelle McBryar
Smyrna High School, Grade 9

Slow and gentle, oh so free,
Our flag flies for you and me.

Our flag stands firm and strong,
And it has all along.

Through the years, during war and peace,
Our flag flies from the west to east.

To this day, and forever may it be,
Flying high for you and me.

The Flag
Blake Solomon
McFadden School of Excellence, Grade 1

The flag is red, white, and blue.
The flag is
Just for you!

America
Brooke Grimsley
Homer Pittard Campus School, Grade 3

Oh America, America, how sweet you are to me.
The red and white so nice and bright stand for the thirteen colonies.

The white stars tell me of the fifty
States of America which remind me of Lady Liberty.

We pledge to the flag to show that we are Americans strong and free.
We'll stand together now and forever 'cause the soul never dies in me.

★

About America

Taylor Espey
David Youree Elementary School, Grade 1

The Pledge of Allegiance means that we are promising that we will love our country and remember the soldiers who died for us. When we look at the flag, the stars stand for the fifty states and mean that our country is free. We stand up for the United States of America because we love and cherish our country. We will pray for the world.

America Still Stands

Ben Hall & Preston Green
Thurman Francis School, Grade 4

The sky is blue,
The grass is green,
The planes crashed down,
But the flag still gleams.
America,
United together we stand.
God bless America,
And bring peace to our land.

America United in Hope and Courage

Scarlett Bond
Barfield Elementary School, Grade 4

Our flag flies proud and true.
Its colors are red, white, and blue.
In the air it waves so tall,
Bringing freedom to one and all.
When the flag you do see,
Stand and be proud like me.

The flag stands for pride,
It's always on our side.
United we walk, united we stand,
It brings courage to our land.
In the American flag I see
Hope, courage, and eternity.

★
40

People will always be okay,
The flag is here to stay.
Red, white stripes, stars, and blue,
Freedom for me, freedom for you.

When the flag you do see,
Stand and be proud like me.

America Unites

Jordan Snyder
Wilson Elementary School, Grade 4

America
We Stand
Today in Hope
To Honor our Country
The Red, White, and Blue

Our Flag

Rachel Runner
Wilson Elementary School, Grade 4

Flag
Our country
Stars and stripes
We come together again
Freedom

God Bless America

Billy Fielding
Barfield Elementary School, Grade 8

The stars on the flag mean fifty states, and the thirteen stripes are for the thirteen colonies. I am glad we have red, white, and blue on our country's flag. I am glad we have freedom in the United States of America, and I am glad that we have a flag in the country. I am sorry about what happened in New York. We will get over it and the flag will be standing forever.

★
41

America United in Hope and Courage
Christina Waltz
Barfield Elementary School, Grade 7

I know we are supposed to write about how we believe in hope, courage, and all that other stuff, but I have something important to say. I used to sit and ask myself, "Why does everyone think the flag is so important? Why would anybody take the time to look at a piece of cloth?" Then after that terrible tragedy, I stopped to think. I thought, thought, and thought. I finally found out that it is made to show we are free, and I am proud of it.

When I say I know that we're supposed to write about America united in hope and courage, I mean that I want to say that I never knew what the flag meant. When I see a flag, I wonder why I did not know that the flag meant "freedom, land and courage." I love this land. God bless the USA.

I used to wonder why anyone would care about a flag. Why do we say the pledge to the flag? After that tragedy it finally came to me that the flag means freedom and peace. Now more than ever I say my pledge with lots of pride. So now I hope everyone understands.

Now more than anything I feel proud to be an American! I found out that this country is better than anything I have ever known. I am glad to have a home here. I love to be able to speak the way I like, dress how I like, be how I like. I wish every country could be like this one we have here. I know we have had our ups and downs, but we are still a great nation.

I love this country and I love *our* flag. I never understood why we had a great red, white, and blue flag, but now I know. Thank you for the red, white, and blue. God bless the United States of America.

America
Rachel Wright
Smyrna Elementary School, Grade 4

America, America, united we stand with hope in one hand and courage in the other. United we stand proudly for our freedom. We unite with each other. With hope and courage we can create a world that is full of friendship, respect, and responsibility. So every time you walk by a red, white, and blue flag, respect it. God Bless America!

★

Old Glory

Tasha Miller
Smyrna Primary School, Grade 4

My name is Old Glory
I am Red
I am White
I am Blue
I am the symbol for
all America holds true.

For those who attack me
they will soon learn
to regret the day
they attacked the
Red, white, and blue.

For behind me are my People
who stand tall and proud
who are strong and wise
united they stand to
defeat evil's plan.

The Flag

Autumn Wilkins
Wilson Elementary School, Grade 4

Listen...
To it blowing
Flowing in the air – soft
Red, white, and blue, standing in air
The flag

★

43

Untitled

Sonia Agarwal
Siegel Middle School, Grade 8

"O, say does that star spangled banner yet wave." These words from the National Anthem describe the present. From outside of America looking in, people see that America is raising its flag. The people have faith in their flag. There is no fear in showing the red, white, and blue. When they raise the flag they have courage. Then the flag shows its colors to the American people and they salute it with their hopes. Americans want the war to end with a victory.

After the attacks of September 11th, people have even more faith and pride in America. Americans show confidence and spirit in the actions they are taking. Americans have formed a new type of trust. This trust has led to security. When traveling places more officers and policemen are stationed for the protection of the people. They have assurance in every step they take. These important factors of faith bring out the courage and strength inside every American.

Every day we have been faced with obstacles and problems, but the courage of Americans overcome them. President Bush faces the truths about America and Afghanistan. Thousands of brave soldiers risk their lives for America. They show their courage by going on secret missions against the Taliban. America's enemies may think America is just a country that pretends to be great, but they don't know the real courage and strength we have. We are united as we stand, and fear will not rend apart this unity. We Americans are continuing our lives.

We are going on with our lives; we still have our hopes and dreams. We have a hope to win this battle. We look into the future and have dreams that this war will soon be over. However, it will not be over until the terrorists pay for their actions. We will serve justice for those who died in the attacks of September 11th.

In conclusion, the flag that soars in the wind carries peoples' faith in their country and remains aloft with the courage and hope of Americans. We are united as one and are ready to prove our mettle. Until we have served justice we will neither surrender nor retreat. We are the Red, White, and Blue that always wave "in the land of the free and the home of the brave."

(United in hope and courage)

Like a big family we stand together.

Breann Holsted
Blackman Elementary School, Grade 4

Chapter 4
Letters

Dear Miss Lady Liberty

Olivia Blondin
Eagleville School, Grade 3

Dear Miss Lady Liberty,

I was just wondering, is it cold out there on that island? Does your arm get tired holding that torch up? Do you wish you could wear another color besides green?

Miss Liberty, I want to thank you for standing up tall and straight. Thank you for holding the torch, which is the light of freedom. Thank you for being a symbol of life, liberty, and the pursuit of happiness.

Your friend,
Olivia Blondin

★

Dear Child
Cortney Owens
Smyrna High School, Grade 11

Dear Child,

I have been through many obstacles and tragedies in my time. I have seen the assassination of President John F. Kennedy, the Civil Rights Movement, the resignation of President Nixon, and even the Great Depression. However, throughout my many years on Earth, living in this beloved country we call America, the land of the free and the home of the brave, never have I seen an event quite as tragic as the September 11 attacks. During my short life on Earth, I have never seen my country, America, become as united as it is now. Miraculous unity has been seen. For the first time in a long time, the Republicans and Democrats are coming together and singing "God Bless America" on the steps of the White House. Americans are giving to those less fortunate as never before. Even children are giving money to help victims of the attacks, and American flags are being flown everywhere by the old, the young, the rich, and the poor. America has become united in hope and courage. Child, not only am I grateful that this season of unity is in full bloom all across America, but I only hope and pray that this season of unity will continue for all generations to come. Now, my child, I am passing the torch to your generation. It is now your job to carry the torch, and pass it down to all generations. Keep the unity alive. For we are Americans, united in hope and freedom, and this is how we shall remain.

In hope,
Your Great-grandmother

Dear Americans
Lauren Nicdao
Blackman High School, Grade 9

Dear Americans,

We truly are blessed to be Americans and to live in this great country. I mean, think about it! We live in America! How many of those living in foreign countries would give their very lives just to say, "I am an American?" God has blessed us to the fullest! We have not had a single war fought directly on this soil for over a century, whereas in places such as Israel, they face the fact that they could be killed daily.

When we say the Pledge of Allegiance, do we actually realize what we are doing? Sometimes, I catch myself just going through the words and waiting until I

★
46

can sit down again. Do we realize that we are vowing our loyalty to the "republic for which it (the flag) stands?" Do we understand that in the 1770's, when the first real Americans fought for freedom, they were fighting for us, too? Can we honestly say that we will defend her no matter the cost? It seems to me that we should re-evaluate what it really means to be called an American.

I hope this letter has inspired you. This is our time to stand up and unite in a way that no other country has ever before. Being an American is much more than living here. It's about being free. Absolutely free.

Patriotically yours,
Lauren Nicdao

Dear Firefighters

Brittany Nornes
Smyrna Primary School, Grade 4

Dear Firefighters,

I am very proud of your brave work on September 11, 2001. You were so brave trying to get the people out of the falling, burning buildings. I am sorry you lost some of your fireman friends. The whole world is talking about how brave you were rescuing the people. The world will always remember your fellow workers who lost their lives. Our prayers will be with their families.

Your Smyrna Primary friend,
Brittany Nornes

Dear God

Taylor Curtis
Rockvale Elementary School, Kindergarten

Dear God,

I know that You are busy, but please help America. And help Afghanistan. Please take care of the kids whose mommies and dads went to Heaven. Take care of the boys and girls in New York and Washington.

I Love You,
Taylor

★
47

Dear New York City

Zillon Russell
Smyrna Primary School, Grade 4

Dear New York City,

I am very sorry about the tragic events of September 11, 2001. Everyone across the country is thinking of your city and praying for you.

I know that if terrorism can happen in New York, it can happen anywhere. I hope that the United States is safe now. I know that there are a lot of people fighting to protect us.

God is watching over all of the rescue workers and the families of the victims. I know that is hard sometimes, but we all need to keep faith in God.

Sincerely,
Zillon Russell

Dear Citizens of America

Jennifer Dusenberry
Central Middle School, Grade 8

Dear Citizens of America,

I have some questions that need to be answered.

Before 9/11/01, how many flags danced in the wind? How many times did you actually listen to the Pledge of Allegiance?

Before 9/11/01, how many marquees read "United We Stand" or "God Bless America"?

Before 9/11/01, did you even think of the Red Cross? How many times did we give blood?

Before 9/11/01, how many times did you acknowledge firefighters and policemen?

Before 9/11/01, did you take the phrase "United We Stand" to heart?

After 9/11/01, how many flags proudly reside in our homes? How many times do our cheeks become salty after reciting the pledge?

After 9/11/01, how many times do we empty our pockets for the Red Cross? How many excuses do we have for not giving blood?

After 9/11/01, how many times do we write thank you notes to brave police officers and firefighters?

After 9/11/01, how many times do we chant "united we stand?"

See the difference?

See the problem?

Yours truly,
Jennifer Dusenberry

Dear Fellow Americans
Melisa Agent
Holloway High School, Grade 12

Dear Fellow Americans,

I've been thinking about our country and wanted to share some thoughts with you. America has really become different within the last couple of months. Everyone is so patriotic and united. It really makes me proud to be living in the United States. I am not really surprised since America is filled with loving, caring people. Everyone has been working together to get through the tough times. We have great policemen and firefighters in New York helping people. We have great people over in different countries fighting for our nation. That makes me proud of our country. We are really united in hope and courage.

Love,
Melisa

Dear Terrorists
Tanner Dalton
Oakland High School, Grade 9

Dear Terrorists,

Victims screaming, phones ringing, babies crying, buildings collapsing—these are some of the sounds of September 11. How you live with yourselves, I don't understand. A year ago if you visited New York, you would have seen the sparkling sunset shining off the windows of those towers. What a beautiful sight! You viciously brought that to an abrupt end. Do you see us hiding? Do you hear us crying? No, I didn't think so. That's because we're not. We stand strong, stronger than ever before. In a somewhat unorthodox way you awakened us. So, if you want us, come and get us. "America - united we stand."

Signed,
The American People

Dear America

Amanda Walker
Smyrna Primary School, Grade 2

Dear America,

Keep our country safe. Help all poor. Let us all stay free and help us. I love you, America! You are the best! Feed little Afghan children.

Your friend,
Amanda

Dear Firemen and Policemen

Adam Moosekian
Cedar Grove Elementary, Grade 4

Dear Firemen and Policemen,

I admire your courage. Firemen, I like the way you put out fires and rescue people from burning buildings. Policemen, I like the way you go after outlaws. You are fierce protectors of the law. I like the way you are courageous. Thank you for giving your lives for others.

Your friend,
Adam

Dear Lord

Christopher Sutherland
Thurman Francis School, Grade 4

Dear Lord,

America is a great place to live, but New York has gone through a lot. We did not expect this terrorist attack.

We will live through the pain of people dying. Things like what happened September 11th are bad.

God bless America. Bless the police officers and firefighters digging through the rubble. Be with the people who lost loved ones.

Amen

★

Dear Citizens of America

Cara Hawkins
Siegel Middle School, Grade 8

Dear Citizens of America,

I would like to offer a note of encouragement. We have recently experienced some severe times. Events and circumstances that we could have never imagined just a few short months ago have occurred. But we endure them as we have many times before.

Our country was not begun without a fight. We had to fight against our mother country England. We had to win numerous battles against the previously unbeaten Red Coats. Our armies were composed of ragtag, scarcely trained militias. Our communications consisted of men like Paul Revere riding on horseback, warning of the impending battles with the British. We fought with our hearts and with a determined will.

Our country then faced a battle of wills. The North fought the South over the freedoms extended to all citizens of our great country. Brother fought against brother. The battles were fought with guns, cannons, and hand to hand. Every battle brought additional bloodshed, but also brought our country closer together. At the end of the worst fighting our country would ever see, our union was saved. Our country was secure.

Our country grew and became stronger. During World War I our country's armies fought in trenches against the Germans and their allies to protect the freedoms of our friends across the ocean. As the second Great War broke out overseas, the Japanese unexpectedly attacked Pearl Harbor. Thousands of Americans died during the surprise attack, but it brought our country closer together as we united to defend our freedoms and those of our allies. Men and women worked long hours in factories to provide our army, our navy, and our air corps the tools they needed to defend freedom everywhere. Once again, our country successfully defended democracy and the rights of the common man.

As the new power of Communism sprang up around the world, we fought on foreign soil once again to defend freedom. We defended the freedoms of other countries in Korea and in Vietnam to prevent the spread of Communism. Even though there was no clear victor in either of these wars, we fought hard to defend democracy, truth and freedom.

We have fought many wars and have suffered through many tragic events, but our resolve has remained strong. We are strong as a people and as a country. We can make it through the events of this day as a people and as a country. We can make it through the events of this day as we have in the past. We need to face each day with hope and courage. As Franklin D. Roosevelt said, "We have nothing to fear but fear itself."

Respectfully,
Cara Hawkins

★
51

Joe Campanella
Buchanan Elementary School, Grade 8

Chapter 5:
September 11, 2001

We Will Not Forget

Jessica Maraschiello
Smyrna High School, Grade 11

It started as a day like any other,
No one knew what to expect.
But as of the morning of September 11,
The world will never forget.

The first plane crashed into Tower Number One,
Crushing many innocent lives,
Leaving many families torn apart,
Children without parents and husbands without wives.

Smoke rose into the air
While ashes cascaded to the ground.
As the plane exploded in the tower,
It made a massive sound.

★

It was the sound of fear,
And suddenly not feeling so secure.
Who was responsible for this disaster?
No one then was quite sure.

When everyone thought it was all done,
They had another surprise.
For a plane was flying far too low,
And horror filled their eyes.

Everyone that watched felt so helpless and small.
They knew there was nothing they could do.
For they watched as the unthinkable happened,
A second plane crashed into Tower Number Two.

That morning all the windows had been cleaned,
And the floors were freshly polished.
A few hours later it didn't really matter,
Tower Number One fell; it had been demolished.

Smoke and ash violently filled the air
As if a volcano just erupted.
It was obvious this attack was planned,
But who could be that corrupted?

As the smoke cleared,
It showed the sad sight of a brother standing alone.
He stood there by himself for a while,
Before letting out his last, exhausted moan.

As America watched,
They knew the second tower could stand tall no more.
People all over the world gawked
As the second tower collapsed to the floor.

It seemed as if America stood still,
Never before had anyone seen such an awful sight,
As people prayed for the lost souls
Aboard those ill-fated flights.

Policeman, firefighters, doctors,
And local good Samaritans rushed to the scene.
Another plane crashed into the Pentagon,
But what does all this mean?

★

Someone is obviously trying to tear America apart,
But we are united as a nation,
We will always stand tall,
With a president of a pure patriotic heart.

America will join together,
We will pull through this.
With God on our side,
It's not a chance that can be missed.

It started as a day like any other,
No one knew what to expect.
But as of the morning of September 11,
The world will never forget.

September 11th A Single Account

Molly Roberson
Oakland High School, Grade 11

    Sudden commotion echoes in the corridor beyond the classroom door as the teacher drones on; the day is typical at the moment. The once vague noises escalate abruptly to an indistinct clamor of murmurs and gasps, but still my class and I are unalarmed. They say children will be children and exceedingly so when together, and the tumultuous clatter in the hallway is agitating but hardly atypical. My Latin teacher takes the authoritative role of disciplinarian, setting his books down and going into the hall to calm the commotion but returns remarkably soon, causing a wave of quiet apprehension to surge over the class. He rushes to the television and as it turns on, it is apparent something is horribly wrong. The ominous baritone of a reporter speaks sturdily yet quickly of airplanes and Manhattan, but perhaps it was the caption upon the stream of words flowing across the bottom of the screen that made lucidity inescapable: America Under Attack. The looming void from the first airplane screamed at us from thousands of miles away as the people on the streets below scrambled and cried to higher powers to save them from this lurid scene. My class, meanwhile, normally a place of gossip and giggles, was for once given to utter silence. I watched in much the same manner as the rest, my mind churning with varying emotions: anger, fear, awe and, foremost, disbelief. We gawk with childish amazement as the newsman points out a black spot on the horizon. A collective gasp is heard not only from us but also from the building as we watch the spot blossom into another plane hurtling into the second tower. The stolid reporter breaks down momentarily as the scene unfolds and murmurs only a choked, "good God" into the microphone. Desperate people toss themselves from the building, led by sheer terror at the nightmarish scene around them that only moments ago had been another workday. The bell rings for class to change, and for a moment no one dares move.

★
54

After what seems an eternity, we move as a conglomerate to the doorway and rush for our next classes — our next televisions. Friends clump together as they hurry to see new developments. I huddle like the rest and receive comfort and confirmations of my friends' feelings being much like my own, when another friend bursts out of a classroom door and looks me in the eyes, saying only, "Did you hear? It fell." I rush to Opera Workshop, an eclectic group of singers, in a state of disbelief. I fall into the already created huddle on the floor and stare on mindlessly once more. We cling to one another, comforting and hugging where need falls; two classmates in particular struggle as they worry about their fathers who are pilots in flight that day. As each receives confirmation of their father's well-being through the office phone, we together let out a sigh of relief. Weak jokes are made in an attempt to lighten the mood, but mostly we clump and watch listlessly. The bell rings again and the rest of the day becomes a blur of reports and blurbs and interviews and talks with friends.

The memory of that day is vivid even months later; the mere mention of it or a picture of the devastation conjures the same shivers of fear and makes me want to flee. On that day the invincibility we once felt shattered like a delicate Ming vase, and yet instead of lashing out we found our strength in one another. When I dig past the pain and anger I find an overwhelming sense of union, among others as well as myself, that I didn't know before that day. Friends became closer, strangers became acquaintances, and we leaned upon one another for a feeling of completeness we couldn't fulfill alone. The world as we know it has changed dramatically, but in certain respects has changed for the better. Flags abound upon cars as I drive; choirs sing; vigils are held. Americans send their money to people they don't and will never know in their eagerness to help. This is the grand scale effect, perhaps, and the media has capitalized upon its wonders and shown it to the world over. Yet when I remember that day, I remember my peers and that clump in front of the television in Opera Workshop when each of us leaned on one another and risked having our vulnerabilities attacked. We learned how to open ourselves up to another person and how to care; we learned the greatest lesson of all in the face of adversity.

Will the Horror Ever End?

Bradley Wright
David Youree Elementary, Grade 5

Will the horror ever end?
Will we triumph or fall?
Will we see light through the dark tunnel's end?
Will tomorrow be the same?
Will there be another day?
Will our tears be dried?
Will hope spread in our hearts?
Will America stand tall and regain her strength?
Will the horror ever end?

★

Sacrifice

Steven Martin
Daniel-McKee Alternative School, Grade 12

Vacation, it seems, is finally here,
I've been waiting for two whole years.
Never have flown before.
Who's that man in the door?
Ah, who cares? Why waste my time?
That man's business is no concern of mine.
Besides, this takeoff makes me nervous.
Oh no, is he going to hurt us?
Why the box cutter?
Why the bloody shirt?
"Has anyone been hurt?" I gabbed.
"Yes, the pilot's just been stabbed."
"You will get it too, all right?
You better shut up or you'll be dead tonight."
Look at that! A flimsy plastic knife!
Would it be too risky? What about my wife?
That man in the window, with the flag on his hat…
What does he want? How can we do that?
Where are we going? What do they want with the plane?
They won't take our money; they must be insane.
Now is the time, this is it!
My heart is pounding in violent fits.
I must do something, not just stand by.
My sacrifice of one will keep so many more alive.

America

Brandon Epley
Blackman High School, Grade 10

We awoke like normal on that fateful day,
Not knowing our lives would change in so many ways.

We dropped off the kids and went to work;
Unconscious of the dangers all around us that lurked.

All of a sudden, we heard a loud roar,
A test of our courage like never before.

We started to hear about all those who died;
Though we may not have known them, we started to cry.

Everyone was scared, but we thought it was done;
Then, boom! We realized it had only begun.

We pulled together, and our nation was stronger;
We could not fear the past any longer.

What happened that day will go down in history;
Who caused all the pain is still but a mystery.

Together at last—"Let freedom ring!"
Is all that the terrorists hear America sing.

America United in Hope and Courage

Annie Pace
Eagleville School, Grade 7

The plane started to descend.
Slowly at first, but rapidly gaining speed.
People were screaming, babies were crying.
The plane was going faster and faster now.
It hit.
Smoke was coming out of the building,
Smoke so thick that people were suffocating.
Brothers, mothers, and sons were jumping out from the building,
Praying they would live.
They were all asking themselves…
"Who could have done this to us, to America, to the world?"
9/11/01
In the future, our kids will only think of this as a date
They have to memorize for history.
But we lived it.
Images of the planes hitting—these will be in our minds forever.
It has changed people,
Made them scared, confused, and hurt.
This date means so much pain to us.
America will stand united.
America will stand strong.

★

America United in Hope and Courage

Jenn Hall
Oakland High School, Grade 11

I was there, right there.
Two blocks away, two blocks away.
From the dust and the people,
From the destitute of life,
From the frantic gestures of mute Americans.
I stood there watching, watching,
As a huge cloud of thickening smog
Took hold of my lungs and changed me.
And still I stood, watching, watching,
As people ran with arms outstretched,
And mouths open, but mine was sealed.
They were gone without hesitation,
Without second thoughts,
Cursed to drift, drift, drift.
Still standing there watching the people
Flood to and fro from the scene.
I took it upon myself to roll up my sleeves.
Slowly and unsurely,
Two steps, three steps, more,
Close and closer, as more joined
The fight to save America.
I stopped breathless, running without knowledge,
And fell to my knees.
For they were in there, Americans,
Brethren, families, and now widows.
Someone calmly said," Why, God?"
As though God could turn it all back with the shake of His hand.
Not willing to pick myself up, someone did,
And with them they carried a small American flag.
People all around me with signs that read, "FREEDOM WILL BE DEFENDED!"
Unlikely vision lets you hope for what you've always known.
Let them take your skin off and see that your muscles drip blood,
Same as theirs, same as theirs.
Let them all see that a flag is merely cloth,
The Bible merely paper,
That love for country and faith
Can never be burnt or scarred.
Let them see that Americans are merely people,
Flesh, bone, mouth, hand,
And eyes—yes, eyes.

★

58

Eyes that swell up with salt and
Release whenever we think too hard.
Someone picked me up off my knees that day,
Someone saw a brother in pain,
Someone helped bear that pain with me,
And that's what they should see.
With the same eyes let them see,
With the same mouth let them speak,
With the same flesh let them bleed,
With the same bone let them break.
For America is still here,
And I am no longer on my knees.

United in Hope and Courage

Jimmy Roman, Jr.
Cedar Grove Elementary School, Grade 5

I am a witness of September 11, 2001.
I saw hate and terror,
I saw pain and despair.
I saw unspeakable ugliness,
But then the smoke and dust cleared.
I viewed love and courage,
I viewed strength and hope.
All of our differences no longer mattered.
Black, white, brown, yellow, and red—united.
Jew, Christian, Muslim, and Buddhist—together as one.
I witnessed the beauty of our nation.
We have merciless enemies,
But we have honorable allies.
Freedom is our greatest gift,
But this makes us vulnerable.
Still we survive.
We have courage,
We have hope,
We have each other.
From a terrible crash of fire and insight,
We have risen.
We are a nation of brothers and sisters,
We are the children of liberty,
And our family is America.
God Bless Us All.

★
59

America United in Hope and Courage
Joe DePeder
Siegel Middle School, Grade 7

All alone, nobody there,
Breathing hard just like a bear.
I was lying there deep under the rubble.
I could not breathe, not even a bubble.
I felt a sharp pain down in my leg,
Then thought of my dear wife Meg.
I remembered earlier when it came…the plane
Crashing, burning, everybody felt the pain.
Then, suddenly, I saw a light,
Yellow, warm, and very bright.
I heard a man yell, "Over here!"
Then saw a face filled with cheer.
It turns out his name was Bob,
He was a fireman; that was his job.
So, that's the day of which I tell,
When I was rescued after the Twin Towers crumbled and fell.

To Be an American
David Pegel
LaVergne High School, Grade 10

The inevitable happened today.

Today two planes crashed
Into our two tallest buildings.
And we watched in pain, in shock,
As others celebrated our downfall.

I think to myself,
Was this a sign of weakness?
Were the towers our strength? Our pride?
Were we helpless to do what we needed to do?

And then everything changes again.
Our pain, our shock, our grief, it changed.
As the walls of the tower cam down,
So did the walls between ourselves.
Our sorrow is might,

Our grief is strength.
And now I know what it means
To be an American.

Now I reflect upon that day.

I must confess.
I felt very little when I heard,
And then I saw the damage,
Saw the wreckage,
And then I was moved
And so were we all.

We all drew closer.
And realized
We are Americans.

That Friday, at a candlelight memorial
I stood with friends that were now family,
Fellow Americans.
I stood between two others, and we prayed.
Then those two became sister and brother.
Everyone in that massive circle became a family.
We were all a family.
One family
A united family.
It was for this,
When my new brother started crying,
As he led prayer,
I held him.

As I walked away from that memorial,
I felt new pride.
My grief and pain grew stronger,
But also our full might.
And now I am ready.
Standing full of pride,
What I needed to stand for the entire time.

I finally declared fully
I am an American!
Since then,
I have not forgotten
Just what it means…

To be an American.

★

It Was Just an Ordinary Day

Kinsey Elliot
Homer Pittard Campus School, Grade 6

I'm just an ordinary girl,
And it was an ordinary day.
But what happened on September 11,
Changed my life in every way.

I can't explain how I felt
When I saw the Twin Towers fall.
It looked like a movie,
But it wasn't that at all.

The fear on peoples' faces,
Made me see,
What really matters in life
Are my friends and family.

I am one of the lucky ones.
I survived that day.
For those who lost their loved ones,
I'll kneel down and pray.

I'll pray that they'll have faith
To guide them through the night,
And that they may find peace
In God's morning light.

I'm just an ordinary girl,
And it was just an ordinary day.
What happened on September 11,
Changed my life in every way.

The Day
Hanna Sparks
Homer Pittard Campus School, Grade 6

The day was tragic.
The day our nation was attacked.
The day thousands of people died.
The day when the Twin Towers fell.
September 11.
The day our nation was shocked, mad, sad, and afraid.
The day they tried to break our nation up.
They failed.
September 11.

How much pain must we suffer?
Isn't it enough to know that some of our loved ones are dead?
Why must we be in agony?
Why did they try to break our nation up?
September 11.

We must stand strong.
We must not let them see our pain.
We will defend our nation.
We will stand up for what is right.
September 11.

The day.

Victims
Ashley Arthur
John Colemon Elementary School, Grade 4

Victims
Frightened, hurt
Screaming, praying, dying
Heartbroken, crying
Angels

America United in Hope and Courage

Diana King
Oakland High School, Grade 9

It started out just like a regular day in the life of America. Bustling businessmen and students rushing off to their designated places. The school halls were full of "hates" and the offices full of workaholics. The nation's center of attention was media-fed controversial hype and scandal. The economy was headed for trouble as signs of recession began to arise. Most people were just too concerned about themselves and the important aspects of their lives, never considering that America could be touched by such terrorism. On September 11, America, as we knew it, was changed forever. The nation first responded with shock; it felt like a nightmare that would soon dissolve into the carefree, sunshine world in which we had lived. But no, it was a harsh, realistic slap in the face to the all-powerful America.

Throughout all the terror and anger, a small light began to glow. This was the light of hope and freedom from which the United States had arisen in the beginning. Such unity began to be displayed. American pride rang in the national anthem and was painted by all the flying flags. People began to gather together, helping each other in such remarkable ways, such as firefighters risking their lives to save others in the rubble. Workaholics put down their briefcases and lent a hand, grudges began to be replaced by forgiveness in schools, and the importance and power of human love began to encompass the nation as everyone pitched in regardless of their situation. The glow grew larger and brighter until it became the torch of the Statue of Liberty, the light of hope that had been the first thing seen by travel-weary, life-scarred immigrants of the nineteenth and twentieth centuries.

After several weeks of tears and hugs, people began to start thinking, speculating on not only the cause behind such a horrific act, but the way their lives were. Some realized that this event has had a small, positive aspect. It helped them realize how unsatisfactory their lives were, what treasured things they have neglected, such as family. They soon found themselves striving toward a goal of improving themselves, giving themselves the courage not to fall where they stood, but to move on. People strove to make themselves and each other stronger, to tell the world that the deceased have not died in vain. The American people and pride have once again grasped the courage for which they are so well known —not only that of unity, but of acknowledging what happened and being willing to put things to right.

America is not a land full of people whose lives only contain gossip and boastfulness, but a land of pride and togetherness, the United States of America. We as a nation were reminded of this when the unexpected happened, the threat of terrorism on the homefront that America had so forgotten. We became united in helping each other in this time of great need, but also reached out to others, admitting our wrongs and how we cannot do everything by ourselves. Life is fulfilled by the involvement of others, in a humane way. Americans, after the September 11 incident, grew in optimism of a better future and determination to not let such evil rule their lives. The strength and unity expressed adheres to the description of our home, "The land of the free, and the home of the brave."

America United in Hope and Courage

Shannon Leigh Parker
Oakland High School, Grade 9

The events of September 11, 2001 stunned the United States. How could anyone have conceived the mass murder of thousands of innocent people? This question rang through the minds of so many. Many were also asking themselves, "How could something like this have happened here, to us?" True, we are a great nation; but, no nation, despite its greatness, is immune to the acts of others.

It was John F. Kennedy who said, "If a man is willing to give his life to take mine, then there's nothing anyone can do to protect me." This has proven true. Throughout history, people who were willing to sacrifice their own lives to harm another have almost always been successful. However, I say that they shall never be victorious. As has happened in this case, quite the opposite has been true. The attacks have brought us, as a country, closer than we have been since the tragedy at Pearl Harbor.

We are prouder than ever to say that we live in America. People have really taken this heinous crime to heart. Flags wave everywhere. Store marquees read "God bless America." People are kinder to one another. We have realized that our lives could be over at any moment, and we shouldn't waste what little time we have here being so cruel to one another. It has been said that after September 11 this year, the world will never be the same. This is absolutely true. This is something that we shall never forget. We must continue to be united in the hope that life will go on, and have the courage to boldly face each new day.

This tragedy is said to be the defining moment of a generation's young life. I hate to think this is true. Generations aren't defined by sitting idly by through senseless killing and tragedy. I ask that this generation not be remembered this way. I ask that this generation be remembered for the firemen charging up the stairs, the people donating money and time to relief efforts, the surge in patriotism, and for all the flags. I ask that this generation be remembered for the unity displayed when danger came. Generations are not defined simply by what crisis they can endure. Generations are defined by their ability to rise from the ashes of aftermath and do something great. This generation will be remembered for standing proudly together and in unison saying, "I am American. This, my flag, represents all that I stand for yesterday, today, and forever. Proudly I wave it, for this land is my land." E Pluribus Unum, out of many, one has finally come to be a reality. Isn't it a beautiful thing?

9/11

Shaleigha Mohr
Oakland High School, Grade 12

On 9/11/2001
My day started out the same,
But on the news, what had begun
Were terrorists crashing planes.

In New York, Twin Towers fell
Because of someone's hate
The U.S. nation gone to hell
Only God can judge our fate.

Bin Laden's name runs through our head
As tears begin to fall
We pray for those who are dead
Screaming "God help us all."

Sirens whirring all around
Black smoke fills the air
Bodies lying on the ground
Some left dazed and unaware.

Children left without their mothers
What now do we do?
Those cowards taking life from others—
Does this seem right to you?

We've come together, all as one
From sea to shining sea
They will pay for what they've done
Americans, forever we will be.

The Strength of America

Carly Davis
McFadden School of Excellence, Grade 3

There was a tragedy on 9/11,
We all began to run and run.
There it was,
A pile of rubble.

Where the Twin Towers stood,
It was all just trouble.

We hope that our President,
George W. Bush,
Has enough strength and courage
To give us a push.

The airplane crashed,
And that was it.
I can't believe,
That plane hit.

There was a tragedy on 9/11,
We all began to run and run.
There it was,
A pile of rubble.
Where the Twin Towers stood,
It was all just trouble.

America United in Hope and Courage

Shawn Pomeroy
Walter Hill Elementary School, Grade 5

September 11, 2001, a horrible deed was done.
Terrorists thought that they had won,
Now they know that war has begun.
People searching through Ground Zero deserve a rest.
Many have died that were New York's best.
Hope is what has kept America going.
Hope is believing without knowing.
It took courage on that day,
It will take courage along the way.
America will have to fight.
We will defend what is right!
So, I hope America will unite!

★
67

America United in Hope and Courage
Rachel Parker
Smyrna Middle School, Grade 8

On September 11, 2001 America experienced one of the worst tragedies the world has encountered. There was a surprise attack on America when terrorists hijacked four planes. Two of the planes hit the World Trade Center in New York, which later crumbled into ashes, one plane hit the Pentagon in Washington, D.C., and the fourth crashed in a field in Pennsylvania. All the passengers on the planes and many of the people in the buildings were killed. Many innocent lives were taken away by the cowardly act of terrorists. America has hope that all races will unite together during this tough time. There is courage in rebuilding lives not only for those who lost loved ones, but also for the people whose lives were drastically changed by this horrible tragedy. America also has hope in eliminating terrorism from ever happening again. I think that this incident has truly changed America forever!

In the midst of all these horrific times America has hope in all people uniting together and helping out. Now is not the time to be racist. We all need to do our part and help each other. If we all could unite together it would solve many of the world's problems and make it a better place.

Along with hope, America has courage in rebuilding lives and being able to start over. Many families and friends have lost someone they care deeply about. They are able to start over because of faith in God and knowing He will take care of everything. Many American lives have been changed since September 11. Rebuilding your life and starting over takes a lot of courage.

Last but not least, America hopes to end terrorism. President Bush is working hard to prevent something like this from ever happening again. An act of terrorism can cause pain and suffering. No terrorist will ever be able to take over America with the sense of unity and faith we all now have.

America will always stand proud, and we will all be flying the red, white, and blue flag. We all need to have that hope and courage during this time and keep faith in the wonderful God above. America is a beautiful place, and it will never lose its courage. That is why I truly believe America is "the land of the free and the home of the brave!"

United in Hope and Courage
Dylan Hagewood
Wilson Elementary School, Grade 5

Crashes, explosions before our eyes,
And now the Twin Towers are in pieces.
People lie trapped, people dying.
This tragedy has people everywhere crying
Left and right—terror is there!
Everybody everywhere is whispering a prayer.
United in hope and courage we stand.
We Americans salute our beautiful land.

America United in Hope and Courage
Kyle Knox
Blackman High School, Grade 9

A brisk September morning,
Everything was calm.
It came without a warning,
What had we done wrong?

As a predator stalks his prey,
We were hit without a thought.
Our family and friends are here today,
Tomorrow they are not.

Through times of pain and suffering,
America, my hat is off to you.
Though millions of us are mourning,
Together we'll pull through.

★
69

American Pride

Alex Winsink
Central Middle School, Grade 7

On a clear, September morn
On the eleventh day
The world looked on in horror-stricken pain
On what a madman's hate could do.

Frantically we watched
In shocked disbelief
At the monstrous destruction
Consuming so many lives.

From the World Trade Center,
To the halls of the Pentagon
To the Pennsylvania fields
Heart stopping pain began.

Though some heroes were born
Some will never be
A great loss of life
Stopped before it began.

On that September day
After we had all cried
We picked ourselves up
And shook our fists to the wind.

"We are American people
We will survive
We will rise above this
We will show our pride."

The world watched with us
In sympathy and concern
Then finally stood with us
Solemnly pledging their word.

Our president was unyielding
The guilty would pay
The American people would exalt
Over these hate-filled cowards.

★

Our men and women stood tall
As they answered the call
And marched into battle
To engage in war.

We must continue our lives
But we can never forget
Though the violence won't stop
Till the guilty pay.

We must hold tight
We must wave our flags high
And show these contemptuous cowards
Our American pride.

America United in Hope and Courage

Niki Horner
Eagleville School, Grade 7

All the people at Ground Zero,
Just imagine how horrifying.

All in a state of sorrow,
Some in a state of joy.

How could this happen to us,
We didn't deserve it.

So many killed, mostly innocent,
It could have been you or me.

They got the World Trade Center and the Pentagon,
But not the U.S.

We, the Americans, are
United in hope and courage.

★
71

September 11
Tyler Morgan
Blackman High School, Grade 10

On September 11, a plain, usual, and normal day
Men and women went to work, and children off to play
America was awake and running, just as many days before
But change was around the corner, as the planes began to soar
Their destinations were common, to fly cross-country east to west
But the result of four flights would cause America to lack its rest
All on board the flight were heroes, with the exception of few
And still many Americans cannot believe this tragedy is true
The New York skyline was changed eternally
Along with Americans who have lost their friends or family
The nation's Pentagon was also a target for attack
We took a hard hit but we will return on track
We all became victims of fright, and some could not cope
But many volunteers stood up and gave America a new hope
Our complacency blinded our nation's eyes
But like the champions we are, we will soon again rise
And the world will see our strong American pride
"Let freedom ring" will be the song throughout our countryside
America was not destroyed because our strong foundation
Built upon God will never see elimination
We are the people of the United States
And we will remain through any harsh fate
We are a stronger country after our recent history
And we will not fall but be filled with unity

Beginning to End
Amy Brockwell
Blackman High School, Grade 12

September eleventh, a time of terror,
Not a normal type of day.
It has bound Americans together,
As we bowed our heads to pray.

Heartless cowards stealing planes
That caused so many to die.
Their act of terror killed moms and dads,
And caused many children to cry.

★
72

The battle starts with police and firemen,
Who for others gave their lives.
It will end when our armed forces
Erase terror from land and sky.

America United in Hope and Courage

Jessica Hooper
Lascassas Elementary School, Grade 8

Everyone will remember where they were and what they were doing
　　September 11, 2001.
Everyone will cry when the war ends, for everyone will be affected.
On September 11, terrorists attacked my country.
I watched the fall of the Twin Towers in horror.
I heard the world cry in sorrow.
Then, as the dust settled and the sun rose, America sang.
It sang of sadness and it sang of loss.
It sang of unity and it sang of freedom.
And with that unity we have grown and overcome.
And with that freedom we have taken a stand.
Why?
Because we are America united in hope and courage.

Now I Understand

Lorenda Pulley
Siegel Middle School, Grade 6

　　The events that happened on September the 11, 2001 were awful, but it has made the United States unite and come together. I could not believe what I was seeing on television. I saw firefighters and police officers risking their lives for people they did not even know. I now understand what the United States of America means to me. It means we all help others and overlook race and religion to come to the aid of our fellow man. I now know that being an American is not just having freedom, but also pride, joy, and compassion for ourselves and others.
　　God bless America.

And Fear With Them

Justin Horner
Wilson Elementary School, Grade 4

Those planes came,
And fear with them!

Those planes struck,
And fear with them!

Those planes took lives,
And we took fear away!

But we did not take away
Our American heart!

America—strong and true!

Heroes of America

Stephen Diaz
Smyrna Middle School, Grade 8

Today, people always think of heroes as famous people. I think there are more heroes in the world than people think. Just because a person is rich or famous doesn't make him/her a hero. Some people do not see themselves as heroes, but other citizens do. Our idea of heroes has changed since the terrorist attacks. My idea of a hero is someone who helps America in good and bad times. The three most important groups of heroes in America since September 11 are the rescue workers, the American citizens, and the soldiers.

First, the rescue workers were a big group of heroes on September 11. They put their lives on the line to save the people who were in danger. It takes a brave person to risk his life to help other Americans. Also, the rescue workers who died trying to help citizens out of the burning towers showed great heroism. People who show enormous bravery, as the rescue workers did, are perfect examples of true American heroes.

The rescue workers were not the only heroes of September 11. The citizens of New York are another group of heroes. They united together to raise money and give blood to help the relief efforts. The citizens who lost loved ones especially wanted to put a great amount of participation in these supporting activities. They all joined together by going to church and realizing how important their families are to them. Friends and family members of the victims participated in many activities during which they placed items at the sight of the accident to show their respect. Even

★

though citizens participated in these activities, they will still remember September 11. Because of the outcome of the attacks, Americans have been crushed at the heart. Thanks to the rescue workers, we are gradually putting together the pieces of our shattered hearts.

Just as normal citizens are heroes, so also are the soldiers who are defending our nation. I think the soldiers who are putting their lives at risk are special heroes. They are taking a risk, but they are happy to do it for America. The soldiers that volunteered were of all ages, which shows that courage runs throughout all types of citizens in America. Our nation has hope that the soldiers will fight for peace and arrive home safely. We are thankful for the people who are in the armed forces for everything they do to protect America.

In conclusion, we should be proud of our heroes, especially the rescue workers, the citizens, and the soldiers who have been helping America out in a time of need. Just because an American is not rich or famous does not mean he or she cannot be a hero. Heroism comes from the heart and is shown by how people care for others, not for what a person looks like or appears to be. These true American heroes should be commended for their efforts during these terrible tragedies.

Attack on America

Taineeka R. Johnson
Smyrna High School, Grade 9

September 11, 2001 will always be a day of mourning in the United States. Unfortunately, this day will become a historic day of remembrance due to the number of lives that were lost. These lives were lost because of terrorist attacks on the World Trade Centers, the Pentagon, and the airplane crash in Pennsylvania. There were four planes hijacked by a terrorist group from the Middle East. The planes were then crashed into the World Trade Center in New York, the Pentagon in Washington D.C., and into a field in Pennsylvania. Theses attacks took the lives of thousands of U.S. citizens and injured thousands more. The attacks have brought Americans closer together. No one is looking at color or race during this crisis.

America's heart has been wounded, but her spirit will never die.

May God bless America!

When the Towers Did Fall

Robbie Land
Smyrna High School, Grade 12

The "Land of the Free"
The "Home of the Brave"
The lives of many soldiers taken
But freedom is what they gave.

The ones that died before us
Have not died in vain.
They sacrificed their all
To take away our pain.

Their lives they gave
To free us all,
But perished were the free
When the Towers did fall.

The unexpected terror,
The horror that did await,
The surprising inhumane act
That decided our country's fate.

The grief in the hearts
Of those who were near
The pain and sorrow
Of those struck with fear

"It can't really be happening!"
"How can this be?"
The words coming from you,
The words coming from me.

In all locations,
All around the world,
People couldn't swallow
What they had heard.

Every ear waiting
To know the cause,
For hours straight
The country was at pause.

★

Nothing was the same,
The cries and the screams,
Every morning someone awaking,
Terrified from his dreams

The country came together,
We cleared our way through the dust.
We came to the same mind
And remembered "in God we trust."

Through the peace we were blind,
Through the smoke we could see
What made us a country
What made us free.

We were all,
We were one,
We stuck together
No matter what had been done.

Let us come together now.
Let us come together all.
Let us not forget the day
When the towers did fall.

America United in Hope and Courage

Kati Walker
Blackman Elementary School, Grade 4

We are sad remembering those who died.
We remember the bravery the police and fireman had as they saved
        the peoples' lives.
We also remember the families who have lost loved ones.
The President said we need to keep calm, and that's what we have done.
We keep in our prayers the soldiers at war, how they are so brave.
We need to remember that we are the United States and we should stand tall!

★

America United in Hope and Courage
Chris Young
Oakland High School, Grade 11

September 12, 2001

The skyline seems deprived this morn,
From my vantage point below,
The sun no longer casts two shadows,
In its growing glow.
My courage far outweighs my fear,
Though I wipe at misty eyes,
I am but a single man,
Though the world doth share my cries.
My teardrops carry sorrow,
As they fall onto the ground,
I remember people screaming,
And the fire's roaring sound.
I try to think of what transpired,
Why I was left alive,
And I realize Christ was with me then,
That is how I survived.
All my friends who died that day,
They are with me now,
And those of us who carry on,
Will turn to ask Him how.

America United in Hope and Courage
Kari Null
Eagleville School, Grade 7

The acts of September 11 have greatly impacted the lives of all Americans. Our feelings of fear and disbelief have changed to an amazing sense of unity. Our nation's colors are flying high and proud as evidence of our love for this great country. After this tragedy, Americans opened their hearts, minds, and wallets. We prayed for and supported all involved in rescue, recovery, and military missions. The outpouring of love has been unbelievable. We can now look past our differences and work toward a common cause.

★

The Spirit of America

Heather Ruse
Oakland High School, Grade 11

On September 11,
America became the United States.
The great Twin Towers came crashing down,
The Pentagon blazed.
People ran frantically through the streets of New York,
Paralyzed with fear the entire time.
The nation came together that day,
The stars and stripes waved proudly.
The blood banks were filled with volunteers,
Rescue workers dug frantically in optimistic hope for survivors.
"The Star Spangled Banner" was heard all around the world.
The kids at school began saying the Pledge of Allegiance with true feeling.
Over a month later,
America still stands united.
Many people are mourning loved ones lost in the rubble,
Others are worried about loved ones fighting in the war.
America is frightened,
But not cowardly.
The destruction destroyed buildings and many lives,
But not America.
The hope and courage of Americans can never be broken,
The American spirit will not let them be broken.
The events of September 11 created a crash that resounded throughout the
     world...
The American spirit came with it.
God bless America,
My home sweet home.

America United in Hope and Courage

Kayce Agostino
Riverdale High School, Grade 11

Chapter 6
United

United We Stand

Gavin Dillinger
McFadden School of Excellence, Grade 3

United we stand,
Hand in hand.

Helping one another,
Working with each other.

United we stand,
Hand in hand.

Every day and every night,
We help one another conquer our frights.

United we stand,
Hand in hand.

With one another,
There is no other.

United We Stand

Brian Blackmore
Roy Waldron School, Grade 7

United we stand
With our red, white, and blue.

With our heads held high,
And our flags waving too.

Justice will be served to those terrorists for what they have done,
Because our freedom will not be overtaken by anyone.

All our love goes out to the families of the victims who died that day,
All those who are suffering know it is time to pay.

We will get Bin Laden for his awful attack,
And let him know that America is back!

United We Stand

Penny Haas
Central Middle School, Grade 7

United we stand
We stand tall and free
To show everyone the freedom that was meant to be
There's no need for bombs
Because bombs can hurt
Just like those wretched planes turned towers to dirt
Many mourn over this so-called war
But it is those who lost someone whose heart should be sore
Stripes of red and white and star spangled blue
Show the meaning of freedom, which Americans think is true
Others show affection by holding hearts and hands
This is what I mean by united we stand

★

United We Stand
Jonathan Seymore
Oakland High School, Grade 11

Here I stand, but not alone.
My fellow Americans on either side of me.
Standing with me, proclaiming liberty.
I will not be struck,
Or moved out of my place,
As long as I see Old Glory
Waving in the face
Of all that threatens to rip to shreds
What our ancestors died to make.
Although I've always been patriotic,
These events have revitalized,
Taking on different shapes,
Tripling in size.
Now everyone has an ocean
Where a river once ran,
And we will now be ready
If anything should happen again.
With the falling of two buildings
A flag up the pole did rise,
All the buildings could be destroyed,
But not this feeling inside.
Courage is the feeling,
To stand in the way of anything that wants us gone.
If our land be taken
America still lives on.
If our lives be taken,
America still lives on.

Life
Stephen Cole
Lascassas Elementary School, Grade 7

Under the flag is where we remain
Through the anger and the pain.
People may come, buildings may fall.
United we stand through it all.

★

The Meaning of Being United

Heather Ramsey
Smyrna High School, Grade 9

United!
Nation that stays together.
Indivisible, no matter what.
The World Trade Center fell, but our hearts rose.
Even in the toughest of times, we pulled together.
Doesn't this mean united?

Tomorrow

Zac Ramsey
Oakland High School, Grade 9

Will tomorrow be the same?
Terrorists struck harder than before.
Will people go in their homes and lock the doors?
Or will tomorrow be the same?
Will we unite to help each other,
Sharing the burdens with our sisters and brothers?
So will tomorrow be the same?

United We Stand

Jonathan Todd
Smyrna Elementary School, Grade 4

United we stand waving the red, white, and blue.
United in our values to be free in America.

United we stand together to fight for freedom.
United we stand for hope and courage.

America United
Caroline Low
Oakland High School, Grade 9

I gaze around the room
Searching for an inspiration
I see none
I rack my brain
What a topic to write about
America
So much has happened in the past months
Our lives changed
Drastically
Anger
Pain
Sadness
Have all become common
Change
My mother says change can be good
Terrorist attacks?
I am confused
How can good come out of bad
Again I rack my brain
Love
Unity
Hope
Strength
Courage
I have found good in bad
Maybe my mother was right

America United in Hope and Courage
Elaine Stephens
Lascassas Elementary School, Grade 8

United We Stand!
United We Stand!

It's what we cry reaching out hand in hand.
We are Americans proud of our land!

With hope and courage we'll find a way
To make it through each and every day.
And in our hearts we'll continue to say:

United we stand!
United we stand!

United
Victoria Worrell
Wilson Elementary School, Grade 4·

America,
Growing, showing, knowing,
Fighting for freedom
U.S.A.
Helping, learning, loving,
Fighting for justice.
50 states united,
Fighting for liberty.

★
85

United We Stand!

Eric James
McFadden School of Excellence, Grade 5

When I look at our beautiful,
Well-worn flag,
I sometimes can't help
But boast and brag.

And I look up above
At the beautiful eagle
The American symbol,
Oh, how regal!

The Taliban forces
With all their powers
Came into our country
And conquered our Twin Towers.

And all the heroes,
How much they tried,
They still came,
Although they died.

All the people that died
In the anthrax cases,
We can no longer see
Their very happy faces.

We go hand in hand
While "united we stand,"
And happily we still live
In the beautiful land.

As they awake a sleeping giant
In the United States,
In honor of our loved ones
The whole country becomes mates.

United Throughout America's History

Brittney Brewer
Smyrna Middle School, Grade 8

When people say the word "America" today, it means so much more than it did months, or even years ago. Patriotism has always been important to our country, but now it seems more important than ever. Throughout America's history, patriotism has soared to many heights and plunged to many depths. There have been certain events during our history that have made patriotism surge. From Washington's time to the present, patriotism has crumbled and risen many times.

In Washington's time, the nation was new, fresh, and unstoppable. Later, although we had slavery and fought against each other, we found a way to unite. Thus, we became known as the United States of America. We were patriotic as we fought against the French and British. We worked together. Women, such as Molly Pitcher, helped the wounded soldiers, and many men volunteered to fight. Together we conquered everyone and everything to become unified into one great country.

Throughout the years, even though it's the same America Washington once roamed, patriotism has sometimes crumbled. There had been no problems on our own land for so long that no one really paid attention. Fights and wars were going on all over the world, and we didn't care because it wasn't happening to us. We never realized how good we had it. Our nation was basically a sleeping giant. It took terrorism to finally awaken us from our deep sleep.

After September 11, patriotism rose rapidly. Our nation had the scare of its life, and we weren't taking it very kindly. We mourned for the dead, and then we readied to fight. We began the fight against the Taliban to win back our country's pride. Together, we would become united again.

The word "united" means together as one, working together. Thus, we became known as the United States of America many years ago. America has gone from Washington's time to today having many surges of patriotism. The events of September 11 have once again united our great country in hope and courage. We will stay like that forever more!

America: United and Proud

Jennifer Hayes
Riverdale High School, Grade 11

September eleventh,
Fear was incited.
Buildings tumbled to the ground,
Yet America will not be divided.

People have always been separated,
But these differences seem small.
We have to look beyond them
Lest we should fall.

United as a nation,
Standing as one,
Whatever the danger,
We will not run.

Because we are America,
Home of the brave,
We won't go into the shadows
Or go silently to the grave.

United we stand,
Divided we fall.
We will stand together
Forever proud and tall.

We will not be pushed around
Or go quietly into the night.
We hold tightly to our freedom
And won't surrender in this fight.

Try to silence our voices,
We will still be heard.
Violence may speak loudly
But not louder than our words

Because when we stand together,
We can take on anything.
Our strength holds us together
And with our stand, hope we bring.

★

Standing not as different races
Or people from different states,
Everyone, stand as an American
To share the same fate.

Remember, united we stand,
And divided we will fall.
We will stand together forever
As Americans, proud and tall.

Unity

Austin Brown
Stewartsboro Elementary School, Grade 8

All my life, I have felt separation.
I had never seen unity in this great nation,
But all of that changed when terrorists came
And filled this great country with pain.

So, while our wounds heal,
God, please reveal
Why unity comes with a price.

We are the Red, the White, the Blue, and the Free

Anne Napatalung
Siegel Middle School, Grade 7

We are truly a country of unity.
We are the red, the white,
the blue, and the free.
The terrorists have threatened
our way of life.
How far must we go to stand up
for our rights?
The bombings, the shootings,
the quarrelling too.
When our children grow up,
will the war be through?
Our country has come together
as one.
We will stand tall and we will
not run.
No man will be left behind,
For in this country you will find
the leaders of the world and
the heroes of tomorrow.
But at what cost? More pain and
sorrow?
We shall walk down our streets
with pride in our eyes.
The smiles and cheers are on the rise.
Whether you're black or white,
yellow or red,
please remember the words I have said.
We are truly a country of unity.
We are the red, the white,
the blue, and the free!

America United in Hope and Courage
Attalie Tobar
Rockvale Elementary School, Grade 4

America is a strong country. It will always stand tall. America has strength and courage because its people are willing to help others in their communities, their towns, their states, and even their entire country. America's people are kind and thankful for everything.

Ever since September 11, 2001, America has been getting stronger and stronger. More and more people are helping within groups or organizations. The Salvation Army helps people with clothes, blankets, shoes, and other necessary things. The Red Cross distributes things people need like food. The firefighters and policemen are helpers, too. America will continue to be strong. It will not let terrorism get in its way because of the hope, courage, and strength it has always possessed.

America United in Hope and Courage
John Kim
Siegel Middle School, Grade 7

Sirens wailing, people yelling, screaming, dying.
The Twin Towers were hit by the metal birds,
And terror struck the greatest country on planet Earth.

As people and debris fell, others came to the rescue,
Saving lives while losing their own.
The fighters died as heroes.

After the dark smoke cleared and the debris stopped falling,
The citizens came in hundreds to help heal the wounded in America.

Since September 11, the country has not been the same.
With war and terror many people died,
But the country held together as one,
United in hope and courage.

May God bless America.

America United in Hope and Courage

Elissa Jennings
Smyrna Middle School, Grade 7

> "The fate of unborn millions will now depend, under God, on the courage and
> conduct of this army..."
> George Washington
> Address to the Continental Army
> August 27, 1776

In light of the September 11 attacks, America has been grievously stricken. The atrocious deeds so heartlessly committed have rocked the nation. Yet despite all the great loss, two feelings that both created and so distinguish the United States of America, hope and courage, have been revived. These two ideas, hope and courage, are not only felt strongly by the country, they are the spirit of the revolutionists and the heart of America.

During the American Revolution, it was hope that kept soldiers fighting on the battlefield, willing to risk their lives. Hope, in fact, was responsible for bringing them there in the first place. Being overtaxed and oppressed by the British, the colonists felt it imperative to liberate themselves in order to achieve their hopes of freedom. After Black Tuesday, the same spirit of patriotism and the love of liberty revealed itself in the hopes that are now felt. Our hopes will keep us standing tall, preventing us from forfeiting to those who intentionally inflict pain and suffering upon innocent lives. Still, the dust from the World Trade Center and Pentagon continues to cloud the sky. Yet,as Paul Eulard once noted, "Hope rises on dust." America *can* rise out of the dust, the torch of the Statue of Liberty shining brighter than ever before. Hope is like oxygen and will keep the fire in that everlasting symbol of America burning, a symbol manifested in courage.

Courage is the virtue that allows all others to flower. From it springs honesty, truth, individuality, and justice. C.S. Lewis observed, "Courage is not simply one virtue, but the form of every virtue at the testing point." Life offers several testing points. For example, America displayed extraordinary courage in the Civil War when she was so eager to do what she considered right that she was willing to go to war with herself. This courage is even more intensified as we have recently been hit by an unprovoked attack. Today is another testing point, another time to prove our unwavering courage to the world.

Hope and courage are not merely two separate ideas that are vital for a potent nation; they are braided together into an ever-spiraling helix, supporting yet spurring one another. One must have the courage to have hope, for hopes can be crushed. If all feared failure, disappointment, or even the possibility of death, then nothing great would ever be accomplished. Hope is one of the elements that lead to courage. It is the desire of a better future that prompts mankind to take action and risk all they have. Without these connections, America would never be what it is today.

★

Today America is a nation that shall not flinch despite the troubles of the world. Emily Bronte once stated, "No coward soul is mine, no trembler in the world's storm-troubled sphere; I see Heaven's glories shine, and faith shines equal, arming me from fear…" This describes America well. The United States is strong, for it is united in hope and courage.

America United

Richard Allen
LaVergne High School, Grade 9

America, America, united and free,
America, America, so important to me.

Suddenly attacked, America grieves.
Despite the weeping, Uncle Sam rolls up his sleeves.

Freedom makes America so valuable to me.
America, America united and free.

Unity and freedom is what we're talking about here,
They cannot be destroyed even by fear.

America, America, still standing tall and proud,
Like its symbol of freedom, the eagle, screaming out loud.

America, America, so important to me,
America, America, united and free.

★

Understand

Elizabeth Hunt
Central Middle School, Grade 8

Is war about the fighting?
It should be about the peace.
Would it take a miracle
To make this cruel war cease?

Would it take a miracle
To make them understand
That killing other people
Isn't worth the extra land.

He may be a different color,
But we really are the same.
It's not that other country's fault,
It's our hate that's to blame.

So remember when you see
Those pictures of those people crying,
If our conflicts aren't resolved
More people will be dying.

How many soldiers have to die
Before the people see
The only way to end this war
Is simply to agree?

Brotherly Love

Jessica Bates
Riverdale High School, Grade 9

As I stand here
With my brother,
Shoulder to shoulder,
We protect each other.
I've got your back,
You've got mine.
A shoulder to cry on
All the time,

Bonded by love
And tightly clasped hands.
We know one day soon this will end.
And when it does,
I'll still stand and say
That my brother
Is with me
All the way.

Love One Another

Loren Lester
Lascassas Elementary School, Grade 5

In these times of darkness
We seek some light.
We want to love each other so,
But it seems like we can't, though.
Let us all join together in love
And root all of our soldiers on.
So hold my hand and I'll hold yours
Because in America we are all ˙
United together in hope and courage.

Untitled

Rachel LaForte
Smyrna High School, Grade 9

Voices ring true, hearts sing out loud.
People hold hands, all throughout the crowd.
Eyes all on her, high above human reach,
Sending her message from beach to beach.
Lady Liberty, you give us our freedom each day.
When we are sad, when our edges are frayed,
We look to you for guidance and in you we find
Hope in our hearts, and peace in our minds.

Acknowledgements

Special acknowledgement and thanks to the
Rutherford County teachers who made this book possible

Sheryl Evans, Barfield Elementary School
Carol Hawkins, Barfield Elementary School
Greg Higley, Barfield Elementary School
Richard Meacham, Barfield Elementary School
Karen Myers, Barfield Elementary School
Karen Hardison, Blackman Elementary School
Tisonya Mastin, Blackman Elementary School
Karen Cox, Blackman High School
Mary Sue Persons, Blackman High School
Beth Sinclair, Blackman High School
Justin Smith, Blackman High School
Carol Haislip, Buchanan Elementary School
Diane Giles, Cedar Grove Elementary School
Shannon Gray, Cedar Grove Elementary School
Melissa Greer, Cedar Grove Elementary School
Stephanie Morgan, Cedar Grove Elementary School
April Sneed, Cedar Grove Elementary School
Wendy Street, Cedar Grove Elementary School
Carol Berning, Central Middle School
Shirley Holt, Central Middle School
Nancy Massell, Central Middle School
Brenda McFarlin, Central Middle School
Tamera Blair, Christiana Elementary School
Patricia Smith, Daniel McKee Alternative School
Suzan Warren, David Youree Elementary School
Marzee Woodward, David Youree Elementary School
Theresa Hill, Eagleville School
Carla McElwee, Eagleville School
Diane Stikeleather, Eagleville School
Karen Garner, Holloway High School

Jeff Duke, Homer Pittard Campus School
Debbie Seigfried, Homer Pittard Campus School
Michelle Strickland, John Colemon Elementary School
Holly Troglen, John Colemon Elemnetary School
Mary Merrill, Kittrell Elementary School
Krista Denton, Lascassas Elementary School
Martha Hopkins, Lascassas Elementary School
Kim Lochmondy, Lascassas Elementary School
Lisa Morren, Lascassas Elementary School
Eloise Rains, Lascassas Elementary School
Mary Beth Walkup, Lascassas Elementary School
Jeff Clater, LaVergne High School
Sarah Townsend, LaVergne High School
Kay Trobaugh, LaVergne High School
Debra Brown, McFadden School of Excellence
Lisa Carney, McFadden School of Excellence
Amy Mayberry, McFadden School of Excellence
Lark Petty, McFadden School of Excellence
Billie Jean Chrisman, Oakland High School
James Francis, Oakland High School
Eileen Haynes, Oakland High School
Debby James, Oakland High School
Nancy Levi, Oakland High School
Patricia Morgan, Oakland High School
Bonnie Tinsley, Oakland High School
Barbara Zawislak, Oakland High School
Maxine Gaither, Riverdale High School
Jennifer Reno, Riverdale High School
Kay Starrett, Riverdale High School
Diane Wade, Riverdale High School
Carol Burns, Rockvale Elementary School
Karen McGregor, Rockvale Elementary School
Jeannie Nicholson, Rockvale Elementary School
Kim Raymer, Rockvale Elementary School
Loretta Hale, Roy Waldron School
Diane Moore, Smyrna Elementary School

Sherry Bryant, Smyrna High School
Holly Gladsden, Smyrna High School
Sherry Price, Smyrna High School
Jill Walls, Smyrna High School
Tonia Drake, Siegel Middle School
Joyce Ealy, Siegel Middle School
Sara Hooper, Siegel Middle School
Susan Lewis, Siegel Middle School
David Summar, Siegel Middle School
Brian Davis, Smyrna Middle School
April Foster, Smyrna Middle School
Kelli Shockey, Smyrna Middle School
Jan Wadleigh, Smyrna Middle School
Reta Barney, Smyrna Primary School
Teresa Penix, Smyrna Primary School
Heather Rowlett, Smyrna Primary School
Margaret Guitard, Stewartsboro Elementary School
Beverly McGee, Stewartsboro Elementary School
Keri Powell, Smyrna West Kindergarten
Paula Lee, Thurman Francis School
Resa Martin, Thurman Francis School
Carol Tomlinson, Thurman Francis School
Sandy Boyer, Wilson Elementary School
Caren Davis, Wilson Elementary School
Annette Hall, Wilson Elementary School
Lynett Kawano, Wilson Elementary School
Cindy McCreery, Wilson Elementary School
Pam Neal, Wilson Elementary School
Lynn Womack, Walter Hill Elementary School

Printed in the United States
3474

9 781931 718158